2011

The New Millennium Begins

Messages for the Present
and
Predictions and Prophecies
for the Future

Art Martin, D.D., M.A.

Personal Transformation Press
A Division of the Wellness Institute

2011: The New Millennium Begins
by Art Martin, D.D., M.A.

Published by Personal Transformation Press.
8300 Rock Springs Rd.
Penryn, CA 95663
Phone: (916) 663-9178
Fax: (916) 663-0134
Order desk: (800) 655-3846

First Printing: October 1998

Table of Contents

Other Books by Art Martin

Being a Spiritual Being in a Physical Body
Journey Into the Light
You, Too, Can Talk to God
Your Body Is Talking; Are You Listening?

Dedication

This book is dedicated to the hardy souls who have committed their lives to clarity of purpose, willingness to accept the truth, ability to recognize the illusions and see the denials that run our lives. To know the truth and accept others without judgment is the path we all aspire to live by.

Acknowledgments

One thought has followed me through life: my mother always impressed on me that I could accomplish anything I set my mind on. Her Christian Science background gave me the support to overcome obstacles which would have daunted many people.

In a 1978 workshop, Paul Solomon instructed me on how to contact the Source. At the time, I didn't understand who or what this Source was, but with Paul's guidance and concise instruction, I was able to make connection with the Source as he described it. With the help of Tara Singh, Ronald Beesley and many other teachers, I was able to access this reliable Source of information for my own transformation. I am so thankful that I was able to study with these teachers.

After the workshops and training, I met Joshua Stone who became one of my best friends and a support in studying and investigating the new world we had discovered together. We spent many months asking questions of the Source. I thank him for his support and help in developing this channel of information.

The Source is a group. There is no name, as they have requested, but I know who they are and what they represent. I thank the Presence of God, the Holy Spirit that works with my Higher Self that indwells with me. I thank the members of the Order of the Jade Cross and those of the White Brotherhood who have worked with me. I appreciate their support and willingness to be with me when I was angry and did not see the Light. I know that I can fulfill the commitment I made to them. They have been great teachers, and I respect their desire to remain nameless.

I am also grateful for my work with Bernard Eakes and Jonathon Leymon researching new processes and locating the forces that affect our forward path. Locating encrypted programs and discovering the way outside forces from the dark side can sabotage and disorient a person's life was a major step, both in my life and the work with Neuro/Cellular Repatterning. I thank them for sticking with me through the tribulations of this research. I attribute their help for shifting my life's direction 180 degrees to a more successful and joyous path. With this help, I got off the final detour on my life.

I appreciate the time and effort that Tony Stubbs spent with me in editing this book and seeing it through the journey to its final form.

Preface

The message in this book is about positive change, what we can do to change the progression of events predicted for the future. *The New Millennium is about total change. The Aquarian Age is about cooperation, compassion, love and forgiveness.* We are approaching the critical mass that will cause this change. Enough people have taken responsibility and committed themselves to this fifth-dimensional shift that what was questionable five years ago will now happen.

Many people feel that once a prediction is made, it is locked in. That is totally false. Predictions can only be made for the hour in which they are made. As linear time progresses, changes are being made by the minute. Nothing is locked in. What *is* locked in is flux and change. We are here to make the changes that are required to protect and save planet Earth from the predicted disasters. We can do it.

As we enter this New Millennium, six major events are happening at the same time. As this 26,000-year epoch ends, a 312,000-year cycle of twelve epochs is ending[1]. The Mayan calendar ends in September 2012. The Masonic Calendar indicates a major shift and lines up with the astrological and mathematical formula from the Pyramids. In May 2000, all the planets will be in the same formation they were in when cataclysmic events happened 6,500 years ago. With the dawn of the new cycle, planet Earth is evolving to a higher plane of existence, ready to make a quantum leap into the Fifth Dimension when critical mass is reached. This will happen some time in the next fifteen years.

The upswing began on August 31, 1987 with the Harmonic Convergence. From 1987 through 2012, all the ancient calendars designate the end of this cycle, too. The Gregorian calendar is the only one that does not end, not surprising since it does not correlate with any of the ancient calendars. In fact, every four years we have to add a day to balance it out.

February 2, 1993 saw a major shift in predictions for the future, and all previous predictions of major earth changes had to be corrected to line up with the new probabilities. The dire predictions that had been forecast are being moderated. And the solar eclipse on February 26, 1998 marked what some have called "The Quickening."

At the end of each 26,000-year epoch, the planet goes through what is known as the "Photon Belt," and we entered it as of 1987. In the past, entry has caused massive earth changes and a pole shift, and many dire, fear-charged predictions foretell what it will bring. The planet also had massive earth changes 12,000 years ago, and 6500 years ago, changes occurred for the first time between epoch shifts. Each time the dark force powers get out of balance, a change must occur to rebalance the energy of the planet.

Each time power shifts to the power brokers who want to control out of greed for power, a shift must happen to start over again. With the shift in consciousness, the drastic and disastrous earth changes have been moderated. Maybe this time we can rebalance Earth planet without destroying most of her population too. This is not the first time the new world order has tried to take over. It has been going on for 12,000 years.

The only people who will be able to handle this shift and the quickening that accompanies it will be those who have committed to take personal responsibility and their power back, and who are consistently working to evolve into this new fifth-dimensional world.

Many people live under the illusion of perceived progress. The true reality will emerge if we are willing to listen; otherwise the only person we can deceive is ourselves. As Pogo (the cartoon character) said, "We have found the enemy, and he is us." Also, many people will be deceived by false prophets—the self-proclaimed masters, teachers, medicine people, and shamans—who claim to have the answers to personal transformation, ascension, and enlightenment. Discernment is essential to determine whether they walk their talk. Very few do, in fact, walk their own talk, and those few who do stand out to those who have the eyes to see beyond the veil of illusion and deception.

This book is about the facts that face us in transition. We are stepping out of the old mold and making new predictions about positive change stemming from the major uplifting of consciousness that began in February, 1993.

The book also examines information correlating the challenges that I have had to overcome in my quest for enlightenment. It seems that the major challenge we all face is to find the truth. I have found that the denial and illusion that veils our sight makes truth elusive. I am always skeptical of someone who claims to have it all together and that there are no more bridges to cross. I am still opening doors in my journey to enlightenment. As I turn the lights on and open the doors, new doors appear before me.

A few chapters of this book deal solely with channeled information, although almost all chapters have some directly channeled information since I do not know where my knowledge, or some information I have read or heard, has been augmented before I actually wrote it down. Most of the book is a compendium of my communications with the Source over the past eighteen years which, once received, was put to work in my life.

Other material received as direct channeling has been presented as my experience since much of it has been given to me in short sequences when needed or asked for; more recent communications are written as received. And yet other material comes from direct observation and experience over the last twenty years.

I have actually learned more from my daily communication with the Source than I could have possibly learned in a conventional college setting. Over the last eighteen years, the Source has always been in my life. Many times, I was not able to hear the message until I let go of my anger, or slowed down. I questioned the guidance frequently, but I found it was always right once I got clarity and was receptive to the information. Whenever I was blocked or stumped by a client's habit pattern, illness, disease, or dysfunctional behavioral pattern, I always had immediate support with answers I needed to resolve the situation. If I was willing to listen, they have always been there for me. I rely on the Source daily and have learned to tell when the information is not clear due to me not tuning in before I attempt to tackle any task.

My body has been through two near-death experiences. The second could easily have been a final death experience. It was a shift in the soul/spirit dwelling in the body. I (the present soul/spirit in this body) "walked into" my current physical body, and the original soul/spirit that was born in this body "walked out." That soul could not handle the lessons with the parents it had chosen, or the life style. He had originally planned an accident that would have resulted in death. I made a contract with the Lords of Karma in which I agreed to take over the body and handle the karmic lessons that were already in place. I experienced coming into the body from the Spiritual Plane without going through the normal birth experience and was able to take the body out of a six-day coma and totally heal it, walking out of the hospital completely healed three days later. I had come in with a mission, but only became aware of that much later.

As a footnote to this Preface, I have recently spent time with Al Bielek, a survivor of the Philadelphia Experiment, an experience that spawned quite a few dreams indicating to me that I was also involved. From my recall, I discovered that I did not return with the ship. I apparently jumped ship during the experiment and my body was cloned, with one version returning to 1943 only to die in 1945. The other version stayed in 1978 and it, too, died two years later in 1980.

As this tale unwinds, we will see that I was a true time traveler, but that I had not achieved the level of consciousness to enter a light body as an ascended being and teleport my self back to my then present.

This is a sequel to my book, *Being a Spiritual Being in a Physical Body*, and a companion to *Journey Into The Light*, a new book of guidance on Ascension. If you are ready to be a world transformer, these books are also for you.

Introduction

Channeled books flood the market nowadays and they all seem to have the same message—that we are the people chosen to make a major quantum leap in consciousness. It's true—we can change our vibration by meditation and prayer and it behooves us to support other people in being lightworkers. This support is very important and will greatly help many people to get started. Yet I see a real conflict in the context of the information being given out. While many books based on research into the correlation between science, mathematics, astronomy, and possible pole shifts/earth charges predict some very real disastrous events in the year 2000, the past does not necessarily mean that history will repeat itself.

Many people need solid evidence to which to attach their feelings. Living in the current state of flux without something solid to believe in can make us very fearful and, ironically, we would often rather have knowledge of some disaster so that we can prepare for it rather than just see the future as some radical amorphous change. Change will happen but we need to know what it is or we feel we have no anchor. Being in a state of flux is safer, but our mind does not accept that premise so, in actuality, the Earth change predictions make us more, rather than less, fearful.

It's great to tell ourselves what wonderful lightworkers we are and how we are going to overcome all the future challenges, but it creates an illusion and denies reality. Many people do not want to take responsibility for their life, so the illusion that someone is going to do the work for them gives them a cop-out. In my sessions, I hear stories about how a spaceship is going to carry us off this planet to some heavenly place where angels or spirit guides are going to clear our karma for us in a mass cleansing with no responsibility on our part.

The reality is, however, that all the indications point to very real Earth shifts, volcanic eruptions, and other Earth changes. Although physical changes on our planet are predicted, we can change the outcome by taking action on our part. The power of our mind is awesome and we can moderate the effects. Planet Earth is a living being and will respond to positive change. As we change, it will follow. The Earth changes are intended to correct the balance of nature and, if we shift from victim to causal agent, we can exercise our divine right to change the future.

Once I attended a lecture where the speakers laid out all manner of dire projections for the future and I could see the audience tighten up in fear. The speakers had moved east to get to a safe place and I could see and feel the audience wondering where they could go to escape these predictions. After the lecture, I asked a few of the attendees what they were going to do. Some dismissed the predictions, saying that such a bleak future could not happen to them and that they were taking all the right actions in their lives. Others blocked it out totally. A tiny number felt they were in the right place and that if they needed to move, they would be guided at the time. I agreed, believing that if we are tuned into the right frequency, we will get advance notice if we are to move. But many were trying to figure out how they could move and get a job in a new location. This concerned me, because in my own lectures, I am often asked, "Where do we go? Where is a safe place?" This book is written for the majority who still hangs on to the old predictions of destruction.

The challenge we face in changing the long-standing predictions is tremendous. We can do it but it will take work on our part to clear the karma that holds us back. Universal Law and Spiritual Principles set out the directions and rules for the necessary transformation. Some of us are listening and can clearly discern the program. Yet others see it as light, love, or angels doing all the work for us, with us having to do little except staying focused on the positive through meditation and prayer.

The fundamentalist Christians see it in the same way but on the opposite side of the spectrum. Yet they are critical of New Age people. Jesus Christ is going to save them when the tribulation comes, and that is the only way. On the other hand, according to the prophets of today, this planet is headed toward major disasters in the near future. But again, the Earth changes *can* be moderated as we learn to listen and to raise our consciousness. God and His White Brotherhood have sent us many Master Teachers during this 26,000-year epoch, and some of us acknowledge the teaching and work to raise the consciousness of the planet now.

Viewing the New Millennium as a beautiful experience with light, love and angels is a great way to look at it, and from information I've received over the last 18 years, that reality is anywhere from 15 to 50 years into the future depending on how we respond. The next 15 years will be a "sorting out" period, an exciting time, and certainly the most tumultuous we have experienced in the last

2,000 years. The higher powers are willing to help us, but *we* must be the moving force to start the action. *We* are the transformers.

Jesus Christ is not coming back in body to save us; we are the teachers now. God and the White Brotherhood have tried to get to us through major teachers, but that cycle has finished. This time, the Christ Force will manifest through us as the message comes through thousands of teachers who have chosen to take on the task of being world transformers. We *can* do it. We *are doing* it now. The "hundredth monkey" theory is working.

This does *not* mean that people are wrong in holding their opinions. Each has the right to make his or her own decisions about the future, and the evolution of our consciousness will govern the future that each experiences and the time frame.

What alternatives and opportunities lie before us? This is where we can apply our training to avert disasters. If twelve clear people can combine their energy in an effective way, what power can 144,000 people muster? This was shown when the December 31, 1986, meditation organized by John Randolph Price grew into an annual world-wide peace gathering each December 31 at 12:00 noon GMT. Now over 500 million people gather at the same hour all around the world. This number can create tremendous change on this planet, as has been proven over the last ten years. Think what we can do if we can broaden the scope from world peace to changing potential disasters.

On the physical plane, the planetary situation is approaching that of Atlantis and Lemuria about 12,000 years ago. Then the destruction took 5,500 years and the legends tell of what happened when the people would not listen. The final destruction of Atlantis took just a few short days. The people had been warned of the changes but did not listen. Many of us who caused that calamity have incarnated today to make sure that it does not happen again. Today, we are not outnumbered by the power hungry followers of Bathar, as were the followers of the Law of One in ancient Atlantis. We can shift the force of destruction and transmute it to love and forgiveness. The more we change ourselves to operate from love and forgiveness, the faster the changes happen. We are the controlling factor. We make it happen when we heal the separation in ourselves and with God.

Many teachers from the Order of The White Brotherhood of Light have been sent throughout the ages to give us the message.

For some reason, we did not comprehend the teachings of these Masters and they watch patiently as we fight and grapple for power when we have all the information to create peace and harmony now. God and His troops sent an illuminated teacher 2,000 years ago but even His own people would not accept him. The Christians call Him Jesus Christ. There are many books written about his travels and teaching, giving Him other names such as Joseph Bar Joseph and Thelonius of Tyana. The name is not important. Who He was and what His message was and is are very important. He said, "You can do anything I can do, and many things better." Fortunately, more and more believe that statement and are beginning to take on the responsibility.

The Book of Revelation by John, another master teacher, is an excellent instruction manual on the process of transformation if we know how to decode it. It was written in Mazoroth, a coded Essene dialect of Greek. The Roman Catholic Church removed most of the writings about spiritual transformation from the scriptures when the current Bible was compiled. Fortunately, they were unable to understand the Book of Revelation so they did not tamper with it. Most of the Bible as we know it has been rewritten by the Catholic Church as a means of controlling and instilling guilt. In fact, the Roman Catholic Church established a "new world order" in 400 AD and held control until the 1950s, when the "shadow world government" took control.

The presence of God is in all of us but most people have the switch in the "off" position. Since the destruction of Atlantis and Lemuria, many great teachers have been sent to give us the word. Some of us have heard the call and are responding to it. The Bible tells us: "Many are called; few are chosen" which shows the control by organized religion over the masses for the last 1,500 years. The correct translation is: "All are called; few choose to listen." (This is an exact quote from *A Course In Miracles*.) This time more people are listening and we will make the shift in consciousness that will bring into reality the New Millennium of peace, joy, happiness, harmony, unconditional love, and acceptance. In fact, so many more are listening now and taking action that it seems like an exponential explosion of consciousness.

We are in the final 14 years of this latest 26,000 year cycle, or epoch. Historically, pole shifts accompanied the end of many epochs. In this epoch, for the first time in history, a tremendous change happened 6,500 years ago caused by the explosion of a supernova, resulting in the destruction of Atlantis. It seems that these events are being foretold in a manner that generates much fear and our task as lightworkers is to turn things around to bring peace and harmony. It can be done.

The New Millennium will usher in a whole new consciousness. The Age of Aquarius began its influence in 1976 and finally supplants the Age of Pisces by the year 2000. The years between 1976 and 2001 are the transition years, and as these transition years come to a close, we are approaching the most tumultuous time. The next five years will see many changes as this era comes to a close on May 5, 2000, a date that many prophets agree on. The accompanying pole shift can trigger either major destruction or very little. As of 1998, the Earth's magnetic field is 19 degrees off true north, and the pole shift will correct this. Our scientists are well aware of these shifts. In fact, NASA satellites use infrared cameras specifically to watch shifts in the earth's crust.

The period 2001 – 2011 heralds a major sorting-out. Those people who are unable to deal with such things as the emotional trauma of their childhood, the transitional changes and the Quickening will opt out, unable to handle the pressure. Earth's population will fall by 40 to 60 percent. After that, changes will subside and the long-predicted "Golden Age" will begin in 2051[2]. By that time, those who chose to remain will enjoy a blissful state of total unconditional acceptance, as fear will have disappeared. It will be a time of total cooperation with no anger, control, jealousy, greed, or competition. No one will need to try to compete with anyone else or take advantage of others. Nationalistic fighting and hatred will be a thing of the past since all those who harbored such hatred will have left the planet. The controllers and the power brokers will be gone. Unconditional love will be the way of life. But before we achieve this New Age of love, integrity, and cooperation, there is a catch. We each must be able to let go of judgment, jealousy, manipulation and control in our own lives, or we will not make the transition.

Self-proclamation will not do; we will be graded on our work by our teachers. We must follow the course guidelines laid out in so many volumes written throughout history. Transformation is a self-directed process but we can't proclaim that we have attained a level of initiation without being supervised. Our teachers work with our Higher Selves and our Subconscious Mind, many times without our knowledge. We would like to believe we have total free choice as we do on the physical level, but when it comes to mastering the higher levels of transformation, we are monitored and, you could say, manipulated like marionette puppets. *We* will not make the decision as to whether we've attained a level of initiation; that will be made for us. (You can check it with muscle testing or dowsing.) Anyone playing the old Piscean game of fear, anger, competition, control, authority, blame and manipulation will be met with: "Do not pass Go; do not collect $200."

No one can do it for you, and neither can you meditate it away. Healing the separation will take real direct action on your part. Being quasi-spiritual will not clear it. You have to build a good foundation for your spiritual enlightenment and soul growth. Once you make the transition to light body, you will not need to declare it to anyone. You will have no need to be recognized. Of course, you *will* be recognized by virtue of how you handle yourself and the miracles you perform. Those who are aware will see your level of enlightenment but you will have no need of their validation.

Unconditional love, acceptance, harmony, compassion, and cooperation will be the way of those who choose to stay and complete their transmutation and transfiguration. When we can manifest these qualities, we will move easily in our light body. All we need do is follow the instructions that we already have. However, most people are unwilling to apply the lessons to their life, preferring to try to jump over the earth plane lessons and focus on the spiritual lessons. Unfortunately, you cannot skip the very reasons why you came to this planet.

If you are willing to follow the course of study mandated by Universal Law, you can move into a light body in this lifetime. However, this mystery school can be quite a rigorous course of instruction. My new booklet, *Journey Into The Light*, gives the basic directions and methods to step out of the cycle of return. It is a very rigorous course in which the steps are very clear and specific. Entering this self-directed, mystery school correspondence course will break all your illusions. Transformation can be easier with a teacher who is adept at the work, and choosing a teacher will test your discernment. Many self-proclaimed "teachers" out there have yet to take the first step in a mystery school, but if you buy into their illusions, they will tell you that they can lead you. It is difficult to find a clear teacher who fully understands the true teachings of the Masters. Many people who claim to be clear are actually being used by the Dark Forces without their knowledge. Many will claim that their information is concise, direct and clear, yet it is coming directly from the alien Dark Forces.

Each time the Dark Forces get close to a total takeover, Earth goes through a major shift. They are wiped out and we start over again. Each time the power brokers are about to gain control and take everyone's freedom, they meet their demise through some major catastrophe. Once more, we are at that point. What are you going to do to support planet Earth so that it won't happen again? You have the future in your hands. What are *you* going to do to change future events?

The only answer is to reclaim your power and your rights, and get rid of the people in government who want to strip you of them. A good example is *Goals 2000*, an education program set up by big corporations and government to shift the educational focus away from teaching children to think creatively and independently to being co-dependent and learning how to take orders. If these forces can engineer this shift in education, our children will be taught to be robots and Big Brother will control children before they're aware it's happening.

The only thing preventing Big Brother from taking over the whole society within one generation is the critical mass of raised consciousness we are approaching. This has yet to reach the fulcrum point so we need to stay vigilant and help people recognize that we're currently on automatic pilot and must get back in the driver's seat. Let's take our power back now!

When we reclaim our personal power, then we can act in our own best interests. This book was being finalized just as the Starr Report was released. For the apathetic American people to have put up with the fiasco in Washington—and meekly pay the bill—shows that most of the population of this country has sold out its power to the establishment. The latter appears to assume that the public doesn't care and therefore it has free rein to do whatever it wants.

It seems that the only people who are siding with President Clinton are those who have something to gain in terms of increased benefits. Apparently, they are willing to sell out their power to Big Brother in return for more government handouts. In the wake of

"Lewinski-gate," this is the question which we must all answer. Are we going to take our power back or are we going to hand it over to Big Brother?

If we take our power back and reduce the size of government, it is obvious that we will have fewer benefits, something that does not sit well with minorities in this country. However, this, too, is an illusion because, if we divided people up by national origin, almost every race is now a minority. This was recently made very clear in a school when a teacher asked the class to bring something to school that identified their national origin. This created a problem for some of the Caucasian children since their families had been in the United States since before the Declaration of Independence. When the children's parents asked the school principal for clarification, they were told that everyone except Native Americans is from somewhere else, so they must trace their original source. The parents countered with the fact that their families had been in this country for over 300 years. However, they were rebuffed and told, "That's the way it is." They took their children out of the school and sent them to private school.

This story demonstrates the *Goals 2000* programming in action! The New World Order seems to think it can lie and disseminate illusions and denials which the general public will buy. It is now time to take back your power and stand up for yourself and your rights.

[1]Various sources cite these cycles and epochs relating to the Photon Belt.

[2]This information came from a session I had with a client in 1981.

1

In the Beginning

WHEN WE WERE ALL SPARKS of light, we could travel anywhere in the universe. We could travel just by thinking where we would like to be. The lights were dazzling, and we experienced all the beauty of the universe, anywhere we wanted to be.

We knew who we were in the beginning. We had no mission or anything to prove, because we were sparks of light, an aspect of God, and co-creators of the universe. Unfortunately, we were not able to experience physical existence, so we decided to drop down into the dense world of physical reality. This was our first incarnation. We were warned by the Lords of Karma and by the teachers assigned to us that we must be careful because what may look enticing is also a test to see if we can handle the *desire state*. We immersed ourselves in the body's desire needs and lost our direction back to our Source. We enjoyed the physical universe, but we were drawn into competition, control, judgment, justification, and defense of our actions. We began to experience anger and fear and lost our direction. The rest is history.

Each time we entered the physical world, we were caught in the cycle of return. We created reincarnation as a process to return to our original state of Grace as sparks of light. When we are on the spiritual plane, we can see the mistakes we made; however, the only way we can correct them is to enter physical reality. We are very aware of the lessons we need to learn on the other side but we lose that insight as we go through the birth process. We have been trying to find our way back for eons.

We go to the Lords of Karma to get a readout from the Akashic Records on the lessons we have to clear but whenever we enter a physical body, we lose the list and the directions. Somehow, we're not able to carry it through with us when we're born. When we look back at the progress we make in each lifetime, sometimes it seems that we go forward ten steps and back six. It seems that the more lifetimes we experience, the deeper we get into the mire of life because we're unable to carry the spiritual wisdom into life.

Each epoch has its main theme. Over many thousands of years, we are getting deeper into power and control—to have "more than," or to be more powerful than our enemy. Hatred seems to be getting out of hand, almost as if it's being inbred in some societies.

We can speculate what happened to the superior race of beings that inhabited this earth up until about 6,500 years ago. Apparently, most of them left for safer havens on other planets or maybe they just returned home to their original star group. However, they left many large buildings as evidence of their handiwork and advanced technology. Could it be that the battle for power became too intense, so they left the less enlightened to fight it out?

Researchers simply cannot understand how these structures could have been built to such fine tolerances by our ancestors with the knowledge they supposedly had. It seems that some superior race took their knowledge with them when they left. Many believe that they left information behind, but it will remain locked up until we can use it for peaceful purposes. Yet other researchers speculate that some cataclysmic event on this planet caused them to leave.

When Atlantis and Lemuria were destroyed, the survivors went to many parts of the planet and lost contact with each other but seem to have retained some of their knowledge, such as the Hawaiian Kuhunas. Their society had no competition or battles, power was divided equally, and they lived in peace until U.S. missionaries showed up. Everywhere the aggressive Europeans went, they plundered and pillaged, and tried to destroy peaceful cultures and take them over. In their arrogance, they assumed other cultures to be inferior, or less advanced. Europe was in turmoil and conflict while the rest of the planet lived in peace until Europeans arrived to take over their land and corrupt their society with their twin gods of money and power.

From now until 2011, this all will come to an end. The planet is moving to a higher plane of existence, from the Third Dimension to the Fifth Dimension. As the new epoch dawns, people and nations must move from anger and fear to love and acceptance, or they will be unable to exist on this planet. How people leave will be their choice. Earth will no longer be the "karma planet." A new planet is coming to this galaxy to be the new "schoolhouse." We will have to "graduate" to remain with the ascending Earth or continue learning on the new "schoolhouse."

We will be "graded" on how we are dealing with the lessons. No matter how spiritual we may *think* we are, it will not do because it could be an illusion. So how do you tell how well you are doing in your progress. First, how is your life path working? Is it full of boulders and ditches, or is it clear sailing? How is your health? Is there peace, happiness, joy, and harmony in you all the time? These are some of the barometers.

Of course, you can deny the problem areas and build an illusion about how well your life is working. The bottom line is always based on abundance of the positive qualities in your life. How intact is your self-esteem, self-worth, self-confidence, and self-acceptance? Do a self-worth inventory (see my book, *Being a Spiritual Being in a Physical Body* for a good barometer).

The beginning of each 26,000-year epoch is marked by a cleansing so that the planet can begin the New Age without negative forces. But each time in the past, the inhabitants of the planet descended into competition, control, and the need for power over others. This has happened over and over since we simply don't seem to get the lesson. However, this the last time for this situation to happen; Earth will go through its final transfiguration no matter what we do. Powerful universal forces are committed to keeping this planet intact for those who choose to make the shift. It will finally cleanse itself one last time of negativity and remain intact in a new reality.

The epoch we are finishing has been controlled by the paternal, or male, influence. The direction in this epoch was a reaction to the prior epoch, a reaction of fear. Any pattern that is carried for hundreds or thousands of years becomes programmed into our genetic and cellular structure, a pattern out of which we react blindly, without control.

Each epoch has degenerated into a major battle for control and the ultimate destruction of ancient societies. Now is a time of coming back to center, being able to act and respond without the need to dominate or control. We are reaching the peak of this reality right now.

The epoch before the current one was under female domination. The major imprint left by the maternal epoch was fear on the part of males of female control over them. It was a very real fear, and one held by the majority of males. Over and over, in my work with men, this fear emerges from the depths of their psyche, so much so, in fact, that I decided to look into this little known aspect of history. The results have been repeatedly validated in sessions with men who were afraid of women, or were having difficulty in their relationships.

In session, I encountered ancient cultures in which all baby boys were castrated before they were one year old except those selected to be breeders, and even they were closely watched to ensure they did not become romantically attached to the women they were to impregnate. However, quite often, romantic attachment would result and the couple would try to elope to some isolated place. They would be hunted down relentlessly and when brought back to the settlement, the woman had to castrate the man publicly in front of the entire community.

These women were not homosexual or lesbian; this was not an accepted practice, either. It was simply a female-dominated society. The males who were not breeders were nothing but slaves. As eunuchs, they had no physical drive, gained a lot of weight, and lived very short lives because their hormonal balance was off.

This has come up many times in sessions with amazing results when we clear the past life. Quite often the man may be with the same person who had castrated him in a past life—an obvious cause for sexual problems with the partner. After the past life was cleared, the conflict disappeared.

I am sure many women would like to deny the part they played in this ancient, barbaric practice, just as many men try to deny that they're acting out of fear to control women. It may be the reason that so many men take up the cause in the anti-abortion movement. And it could explain why the religious right wants to keep women in bondage. Simply put, they are afraid of them. It may also explain the women's liberation movement.

Recent years have seen an epidemic of breast cancer in women and prostate cancer in men. This gender issue seems to be becoming a very intense situation with people for whom the issues of power and control are important. The "dis-ease" of perceived loss of power in men and rejection of the feminine role in women seem to be settling in these areas of the body. Society seems to be losing a clear gender identification.

The authority figure issue seems to be more of a problem for men than women. With women, the issue comes up for those who are, or want to be, in positions of power and control. It can also happen when women reject the female identification placed on them by society and the conservative fundamental religious community that want to limit women to the home-maker/mother role. The oddity in this is that gay women tend not to suffer this cancer epidemiology. Women will deny that they are rejecting the female role model, but the mind will revert to the past programming and put itself in a double bind. This is not, of course, to say that women cannot hold positions of authority and power or step out of their traditional role.

In cases such as this, hopefully a woman can make peace with the sub-personalities that are holding a social/religious model that places the female role in a subservient position. A new program that allows women to naturally assume positions of authority must replace the traditional societal role model. However, during this replacement process, women must be clear so that there is no internal conflict with gender identity.

Prostate cancer seems to show up in men who are unable to claim their personal power and feel that women are taking their power away. Quite often, this is complicated by men denying their feelings. Men who cannot accept that they are threatened by women in authority can go into denial which, in turn, causes prostate cancer. Most men react to issues of power and authority at the survival and sexual level. The "macho man" sees himself primarily as a physical being, his body being his identity. If he is competing with women at work, he sees this as fighting for his superiority. Women in authority threaten him, and if he has a woman boss, he feels as though he has lost a large part of his identity. Matters are further complicated if he had a domineering, controlling mother. Until he can accept all people as equal, such a man can be living an unnecessarily complicated life.

This is not to make a judgment of any person, male or female. My work has shown that the soul will carry forward unresolved past life issues until we clear them. The past can be cleared very easily by recognizing the lesson and claiming Grace. When you do this, you can forgive yourself for participating in the activity in that life, plus any harm your activities caused.

There can be no denying the abuse of women by men over the past 26,000 years. A lot of the anger may have been acted out in subconscious reaction to their treatment from the prior epoch. Women are also reacting to their treatment in the current epoch. But we must view all past lives and their effects on the present in context. We cannot look at one incident and make a judgment about past or present. When we view the continuum of life in the macrocosm and see the big picture, we can piece together the puzzle and understand the situation.

Buried deeply in the gender issue is the role of freemasonry in the formation of societies on this planet. The founders of the United States of America were all members of the Masonic Orders—in fact, Washington was a Lodge Grand Master. The majority of U.S. presidents were freemasons up through Harry Truman. Since 1952, only one president, Gerald Ford, was a freemason. What does this tell us? It is quite obvious that the power started shifting with the onset of World War I. The battle for power began and has continued up to the present.

My father was a freemason and wanted me to join Demolay, the young men's branch of the freemasons, but I did not. Long ago, as I read a book about the battle of the masons within the Catholic Church., I started to pass out and I could feel fear rising through me. In hindsight, I realized that I had been involved in this battle and have been killed by the church in many lifetimes.

One of the greatest planetary powers over the last 1,000 years and one that still reigns as a world power is the Roman Catholic Church, or the "New World Order." In the past, the battle for power was so intense that there were times that people had no freedom at all. In the name of God, the Catholic Church tortured and killed millions of ordinary people simply because they stood up for their freedom.

In researching the role of the Catholic Church, I discovered the origin of the name Demolay. Apparently, Demolay was a Frenchman and the head of the Knights Templar (a branch of the Masons). He was burned at the stake because he would not back down to Pope Clement and King Philip of France. As he died, he cried out to them, "You will both die a traumatic, painful death within the year." They both laughed, celebrating their destruction of the Knights Templar. King Philip died three months later, and Pope Clement six months later, both from painful and traumatic causes. Karma was immediate in this case.

The Roman Catholic vendetta against the freemasons is well documented. Also, the Roman Catholic Church led the new world order movement from about 325 AD to 1950 when a new group took over. North America was settled by people trying to escape the power of the Church, but now we have the new world order and a corrupt federal government to contend with. Where can we escape to now? There are no new worlds to flee to so we must change where we are. Fortunately, critical mass will shift the order.

The pendulum has swung from side to side for many thousands of years. The New Millennium will bring the pendulum to the center, with cooperation, forgiveness and unconditional love prevailing. We have one final chance to get it right. We either flow with the changes or we miss the transfiguration and pass on to incarnate on the new work planet, back into the cycle of return.

We were all sparks of light in the beginning. We will all return to that point sometime in the future. How many years or millennia it takes is our choice. The cycle of return will continue until each soul in the universe makes it back home to a spark of light. At the rate we are going, it will take many thousands of years. This does not mean that those of us who have made the choice to stop the return cycle in our lives will be held back. Nobody can hold you back in this home study course. It is a correspondence course. Our teachers are ready. All we have to do is indicate our readiness to step on the path.

As we begin to accept the lessons and move up our path to ascension, we teach by example. I know of only three people who have completed the process. Only one has come back to teach what it is all about. Very few are listening to him. Even when a number of us enter light bodies and people can actually see what is required, most people will still deny the reality.

Many people who talk about and teach ascension are barely on their own journey, so much of what they teach is pure speculation. When these teachers can demonstrate that what they teach works, we will have a process that we can follow. Many people have made outrageous claims that they have ascended and have come back to teach. Yet when I look at their records, I see no one who has been validated by the teachers of the Brotherhood of Light in the Akashic Records. Of course, the records are open to anyone, including you, with no special password or connection required.

Teachers will appear to help us when we indicate our intention to transform. The Holy Spirit and members of the White Brotherhood are at our elbow, ready to help. They observe our progress but have no vested interest in how we learn our lessons, or how long it takes us to achieve the end result.

In this matter, there is no "free" will; the program is not optional. But we each have the choice of being on the field of play or opting out and returning to the cycles of reincarnation. There never was any free will. The plan has always been that each time we took on a body, we were to learn the lessons and follow the directions we drew up before birth. When we get in the body, we seem to lose the instructions, the road map, and the directions.

Since we have the free choice to do whatever we please, we often get caught in the downward spiral of competition, control, authority, manipulation, and being victims of the world around us. We can cop out in the illusion and can blame someone, or the situation. But we have created it all; we choose the karma and how it is played out. More and more people are recognizing this and managing to pull out of the downward spiral.

I don't believe for a second that I have the process delineated and laid out in full. But from observing the people I've worked with and their progress, I believe that I am on the right track. I gauge my work by my progress, and since 1994, I am beginning to achieve the goals I set many years ago. It has been a long haul. I never dreamed that I would have to battle with the Dark Forces. Very few people are willing to take on the Dark Forces and follow through. Fortunately, most people fear them or they just deny that they're a real threat. I have discovered that they are *very* real but that we can overcome them.

The Orions, the Dracos and the rebellious Pleiadians and Andromedans are working with fourth-dimensional astral and demonic entities. Their mission is to stop the fifth-dimensional jump and prevent critical mass from being reached. If they can achieve their objective and stop the resonant frequency of the Earth's magnetic field from rising above 10.5 hertz, they will have succeeded. The planet will tumble into the Fourth Dimension and they can take over. But we will not stumble because we are now forcing the aliens back to their home planets.

We're on the runway ready for takeoff. Are you ready? We will mitigate any devastation that the predicted Earth changes and the pole shift will cause. We have it in our power. Our actions and response to the present pattern will decide how we survive in the near future. We have only until about 2001 to learn the lessons. However, we have a lot of help waiting for us, so avail yourself of the support. Just ask with the proper language and you will get it. The tools and the path are all laid out; all we have to do is follow the instructions laid out for us in the Akashic Records. My book, *Journey Into The Light*, lays out the process and steps in transfiguration that open the doors to ascension.

2

The Role of
the Prophet

THE ROLE OF A PROPHET is to bring future information to the forefront so that people can become aware of it. It is then up to the people to weigh the information and heed the warning. All the lectures, workshops and tapes to which I have listened generate a great deal of fear, with very little prognosis of what a person can do. The negativity caused by the fear will actually bring a prediction to fruition because fear gives energy to the outcome. Anger and fear are very strong catalysts; they can siphon vast amounts of energy from unrelated areas and people with no knowledge of each other, collect it on the emotional plane, and unleash it as a moving force.

Many of the intuitive people making these predictions have good intentions and, while much of their information is accurate and correct, if you have a flaw in your clarity, a Dark Force being can jump in as has happened to me. Some of the information concerning total destruction of populated areas comes from the Astral Plane and the Dark Forces who are bent on destruction of this planet. They want a home planet, so they have a vested interest in seeing this planet cleared in order to take over. The Astral Plane houses tremendous pent-up anger so that the earthbound beings there feel trapped. Illusion exists in the Astral, just as it does in the Third Dimension but if only they could rise above it and move on to the spiritual plane, they could clear their anger.

As with any information, we have to be clear who is talking to us, sending us visions or communications. My experience over the last 20 years has taught me that countless inter-dimensional beings co-exist with us, all around us, all the time and that they are trying to break through to misdirect and control us. In fact, so much intensity has built up over the last ten years that, at one point, I

11

wondered if we would survive the onslaught of this negative Dark Force energy. However, the Source told me that it would peak during the last six months of 1995 and that the Dark Forces would depart by the beginning of 1996.

Around January, 1996, I did indeed notice a considerable drop in astral activity and by 1998, the alien intrusion seemed to have ended. The Intergalactic Council also verified that the Orions and Dracos had pulled back but we did not account for a rebellious, criminal Orion faction that hid behind an illusory retreat as they continued to work through the fourth-dimensional Dark Forces. Rebellious Pleiadians also continue to support the Orions.

This all came to a head when I discovered that, as an electronic technician in a past life, I was one of those who broke into the Akashic Records many thousands of years ago. We set up a computer network so we could track people and control them by implanting a "tracker chip" in them. It turned out that I was the only one of twelve who had jumped ship and deserted the alien Dark Forces.

When I renounced and revoked my allegiances to them and switched allegiance to the Light, the Orion forces began trying to destroy me. For many lifetimes, they had put all manner of curses, hexes and spells on me that we have just finished clearing. We also discovered I had the computer access code to the Orion computer network. We gave it to the Forces of Light so they could jam the Orion computer network, or infect it with a virus. The Orions shut down their computer network and disappeared in less than five minutes. So in August 1996, the Orions finally departed planet Earth. We did find a band of rebellious Pleiadians who tried to reactivate the system, assuming they could slip in unnoticed. There have been no intrusions by the Orions since then.

Unfortunately, it seems the rebel aliens are not ready to give up. As soon as the Orions left, the rebel Pleiadians moved in and we had to contend with them until January 1998, when we thought we were home free. We did not expect an onslaught by another alien group.

The Intergalactic Council assured us that when an alien group moves into the third dimension for more than ten to twelve months they will assume that frequency. They explained that higher dimensional beings cannot operate in a lower dimension continually without lowering their frequency to that dimension. Since they were operating with the dark forces in the fourth and third dimension, they would lose their higher dimensional powers. Many of the Pleiadians recognized this, retreated, and returned to their home planet. Those who remained became a part of the dark forces with their knowledge, but not their powers.

We had asked the Pleiadian Command many times if they could take care of their own people who were harassing us. Their answer was that they are not the intergalactic police. The Sirians replied in the same manner. Apparently they felt it was our lesson since we attracted these people to our planet and taught them how dishonest, unethical people function. Being in our dimension caused them to lose their integrity. They got caught in the same behavior that caused all of us to lose our direction and stray off the path.

This is a major lesson for us. The Book of Revelation describes what can happen when one gets caught up in the energies of the lower beast. It makes no difference where you are if you get dazzled by power and control, trapped by the compulsion and obsession to take over.

Apparently, the Pleiadians were replaced by the Andromedans to continue the battle with the dark forces. The difference with Andromedans is that they are much more technologically advanced. They don't use implants at all, but have much more effective ways to control people. They can get directly into the human mind and set up new programs. They can literally take possession of your mind and set up programs that control how you function.

Their favorite approach is to set up disease programs in the neurological system, such as Chronic Fatigue, Epstein-Barr, MS, ALS, and MD. They can also disrupt the immune and endocrine systems. They can set up a belief in the middle-self about the program so that the body follows the instructions. After a while, the program will actually cause the disease to manifest. They can also disrupt the body's electrical system. This has happened to me personally many times. I have to delete, erase and destroy the program and the operating instructions. Then the symptoms disappear within a few minutes.

Dealing with these aliens is much more complex because we have to figure out what they are up to before we can clear the program. To complicate matters, the programs can hide in many forms and even deactivate themselves to avoid being located. A favorite trick is to take over a sub-personality, assuming its behavior, so that the program cannot be found.

However, in a dialogue with the Intergalactic Council, we were informed that, as with the Pleiadians, the Andromedans will lose their power by the end of September, 1998. This actually came to pass in mid-October, 1998, when the last of the Andromedans left.

There will be deceivers among us. When religious elders used to say that the Devil or Satan can do the same works as the Christ, I tended to believe they were wrong. Why would God give all the good things to the Devil? However, in 1997, I changed my mind, having seen some miracles that were performed by people aligned with the Dark Forces. The Anti-Christ forces are among us but, fortunately, we have tests to identify them.

It seems that, quite often, people who make predictions need to be right—their only validation is to be right. But with the mass consciousness changing so fast, it is very hard to make a prediction that will apply beyond the particular day you make it.

A projection is simply a probability. As long as the event has not come to pass, it is still only a probability. If the prediction does not happen, the consciousness change (which is moving at an ever-increasing rate) probably averted the incident. Some people make predictions as if the events are already locked into some inevitable future in which we have no choice. In the past, however, this has proven to be untrue.

Many people give credibility and a considerable amount of energy to all the disasters that were supposed to happen during the last decade of the old millennium. Most of the predictions have not actually happened, but to survive the predicted future calamities and disasters, we must take specific, very committed action. Not only do we have to clear all our fear of the future but we have to recognize and even welcome this time of transition. There is no blame, and there are no victims. We set this all up to understand the lesson. Some of it is group karma, but most of the individual experiences we are going through are our own personal karma. We must accept total and full personal responsibility to let go of our anger, judgment, control, manipulation, blame placing, and responsibility avoidance. This book will stress this all the way through—nobody else can or will do it for you.

The past 20 years have seen many books about the coming Earth changes, the best known being by Edgar Cayce and Nostradamas. And in 1980, John White wrote *The Pole Shift*—a well-written compendium and collection of basic information from the scientific perspective and from the views of many major prophets, intuitives, clairvoyants, and mediums.

Many prophets proclaim disaster for the West Coast of the U.S., so let me balance the Doomsday predictions with the bright side of the new messages that have come to me over the past few years. I feel that this has changed with the uplifting of a personal consciousness.

The West Coast is a breeding ground for new ideas, awareness and movements at all levels; there is nothing static about the west. It seems odd that the areas where there is very little consciousness uplifting would be considered safe since all the disastrous changes of the past epoch have hit the areas where the population was most concentrated and the fight for power, greed and corruption was rampant.

Most of the disasters today are not happening on the West Coast. Where are the floods, hurricanes, tornadoes, and great fluctuations in winter weather happening now? The West Coast has had its share of disasters with El Nino in the Spring of 1998, but they do not continue all year.

Many people coming from the East can feel the change as they pass through Nevada and Arizona into California, Oregon, and Washington. Most feel that the West Coast is almost a different country. It follows that if the disasters are going to strike the West Coast as predicted, disastrous weather would also hit. My information is that disasters will strike the areas where consciousness is not evolving, areas where the overwhelming forces are fear, anger, greed, control, competition and the need for authority.

This is not to say that earthquakes will not hit the West Coast. There will be floods, quakes, and tidal waves for sure. Where are the disastrous hurricanes, tornadoes, floods, severe freezing weather, and earthquakes hitting? If the West Coast of the U.S. was to be the focal point of the destruction of the land mass, more problems would be apparent. I am told that it will all come to a different end as we move into the new millennium.

I am taking a bold step in my new predictions (see Chapter 3). Initially, my predictions aligned with all others of which I was aware. No significant change over the past 50 years in the predictions for the Earth Changes suggested to me that they would happen as projected. But now I feel this is out of step with new consciousness. While there will be significant earthquakes and other disasters, I now see that they will be much less severe to the land mass and the environment than predicted in the past.

Already we have averted many earthquakes by future progression and remote viewing. A committed group of people acting to subvert an earthquake shows us that we can use the positive effect to *stop* a disaster in the same way fear would *cause* a disaster.

I have seen over the years that when we lock in predictions in print and on maps, we actually give energy to the predictions and fuel them into action. This illusion of mass consciousness will cause people to precipitate their feelings, fears, and thoughts into a solid force that could bring about the very situation they fear. When enough people focus power, it can cause something to happen, positively or negatively. We give away our power to authority figures, then we react to sensory input unconsciously. If we are not monitoring our mind's self-talk, fears will come up without our knowledge of their origin. We will then act on those fears, creating a massive flow of energy into that fear. When that energy reaches a critical mass, the belief will cause an event to take place. So why not focus on the positives rather than on the negatives?

On February 2, 1993, a major shift occurred with the astrological conjunction of outer planets in Capricorn. This caused a major directional change of energy to a more positive turn and changed the basis for all predictions. We also now have help from the Sirians and the Pleiadians, who don't want this planet to blow out as Mars did.

Although many focus on the old information passed down through the centuries, the old Piscean behavior patterns will not work after the year 2011. We must shift to an understanding of cooperation, compassion, joy, harmony, forgiveness, and unconditional love.

With self-proclaimed spiritual teachers, shamans and medicine people on every street corner, we must use spiritual discernment to find the pearls. Most have some valuable information to share, but many are very believable spinners of illusion. The real test is whether they have a need for control and outside validation. How effective are they in guiding their students? How successful are their students in finding peace, happiness, harmony, joy, unconditional love, and wellness in their lives?

We must be very careful about whom we listen to. It would be best for you to get your own phone line connection to the Akashic Record, with your Higher Self as the operator. It is very important to get a good relationship with your Higher Self before you start "surfing the net" looking for a Spirit Guide or a Source to talk to. Once you connect to your Source, you can tune into everything available. The Highest Source of your being is your telephone operator to the universe.

Connecting to Your Source

Entering the inner planes without a guide can be dangerous. Many people just open indiscriminately to anything that comes along. Safely venturing into the realm of channeling without a specific reference point to start from requires great discernment. In the past few years, so many Dark Forces from all levels have been trying to misdirect people that we need all the tools available to ensure that we are in contact with a being of the light.

In my training, Paul Solomon always stressed asking who we were connecting with and to make sure they identified themselves. Universal Law requires that when you ask an entity to identify itself, it must do so honestly. I have found the negative beings will rather depart than identify themselves. Fortunately, the Dark Forces of the alien extraterrestrial world have been told by the Intergalactic Council to pull back from planet Earth, but we still have to contend with demonic and inter-dimensional beings from the Astral Plane. When we check to see if a person is controlled by Dark Forces, we find many who were clear at one time but are now controlled by inter-dimensional beings with dark overshadows. They enter insidiously and are almost impossible to detect.

When you desire to get to a point of clarity with safety, it is best to call on a guide to help you across the Astral Plane. When you are reaching out to a higher being, raise your vibration to connect with a fifth-dimensional or higher being. However, lower beings can lead you astray and convince you that they are high beings. The Dark Forces have no ethics or integrity, and their main weapon is your willingness to believe—it can cause you to be gullible. Be careful!

Going across the fourth-dimensional plane without protection can be dangerous. The only safe way I have found is to call upon the Higher Self, Holy Spirit, Presence of God, and Guardian Angel to guide me over. There are deceivers at every corner, but this affirmation will carry you over to the Fifth Dimension and open the door:

As the Christ Master Self that I am,

I am totally committed to enter into contact with the Highest Source of my being,

I ask you, my Higher Self, Holy Spirit, Presence of God and My Guardian Angel,

To guide me into the Highest Source of my being,

I am entering your presence now

At this point, you are into the Fifth Dimension and can ask to communicate with any being on this dimension or above. The Highest Source of your being will connect you.

This process eliminates all the spirit guides from the lower dimensions who are looking for a mouthpiece. Many of them feel alone, lost on the Astral Plane or earthbound, so they want to talk to somebody. They set themselves up with a fancy name and look for a person who is open to let them come through.

Many times they have been recruited by the Dark Forces and will follow their instructions to taint information very subtly so that it will sound accurate but there will be a twist in it to misdirect. Fourth-dimensional beings may have been on the Astral Plane for thousands of years, so they are very good at pulling in a lost person and offering many benefits for working with them.

There are no ethics, integrity, or need for honesty on the Astral Plane—entities will masquerade as anything they choose. They will tell you anything you want to hear. If you buy it, it lets them off the hook. If you command them to reveal their true identity, they have to do so. Discernment is the key to being able to connect to a reliable source from The White Brotherhood.

1996 was the year of clarity in which we were forced to clear all vows, oaths and allegiances we carry from past lives. We also found many curses and hexes that had been placed on people in past lives. Often demonic spirits were attached to these curses and hexes to enforce or control them. Sometimes, they were three to seven levels deep, depending on your activities or connection with the Dark Forces or the Roman Catholic Church in past lives. It is very hard to be a clear channel if you are carrying these demon spirits.

Do not delude yourself into thinking you are clear without being checked and cleared. These entities love to push you into self-righteousness. It gives them a real kick to think they can control you without you knowing it. Their whole existence is dedicated to deception, control, manipulation, and destruction. Their mission is to convince you that they do not exist, or that they are an illusion, while controlling and manipulating you. The Dark Forces do exist, even if we choose not to believe that fact. Thus most of their activities go on without detection by the average person.

How Will the
Future Unfold?

IN ALL MY DISCUSSIONS WITH Source since I began communicating with them in 1978, they have stated that all information was subject to change, or modification, depending on the outcome in the future. Every prediction was merely a probability until it had actually happened. In understanding human psychological behavior and the process of transformation, they have been very accurate. Many predictions on political or financial activities have not come to pass and they always explain the reason for the outcome, and why it happened in that manner.

If you were to look at what is written in the Akashic Record at this time, you would see that traumatic disaster predictions are still in place. Many people are involved in remote viewing of the "collective unconscious" as they describe it. Remote viewing can only access what is written in the Akashic Records.

Many people tap into the records psychically, or with visions, and dreams but when using this method to view the records, they can only pick up what is written in that specific time frame. If it has not been updated, then they may see old, outdated predictions. Each time a critical mass in consciousness is reached or a new event happens with a Quickening of the time frame, the records are updated. The update may change or even erase the pattern of a predicted event, such as an earthquake that does not take place because of the raising of consciousness in the area. The critical mass has affected the prediction. Major events will be changed by people increasing their awareness or heightening their consciousness. The Quickening calls for us to evolve at an ever-increasing rate, building to an astounding rate of movement.

Quite often, I find that I am on the cutting edge of new events because I do not tune in to old energy or old dialogue. I will look at the Akashic Records to see what the current predictions are for the future but I do not go by the present records or the probabilities, or by dreams or visions. Almost all of my communication is direct dialogue in a non-trance state. As a result, it is a conversation in which I can ask questions and, at times, contest the information. If I disagree with the Source, they will always explain their theory or reasons why it is given.

The dialogue that I have with this group of evolved Souls shows clearly that they are overseeing the future as it may come to pass, and viewing the probabilities. They evaluate the critical mass required to change an event and weigh the evolution taking place. When I later ask why an event did not happen, they give me the reasons which I can usually verify from conventional news sources. Sometimes the critical mass moves so fast that it changes the event in a few days or even minutes.

The remainder of this chapter is directly channeled material from the Source.

Closing the Chapter

As we bring this chapter of human existence to a close, we have to focus on one avenue. In 1987, you entered into the last days of your time on planet Earth. By this, we mean that you have to make a choice: do you want to remain on this planet as it makes its shift to the Fifth Dimension, or will you leave for the new working planet?

As theoretical time speeds up or "quickens," you will notice people who feel the shift to the point that it will upset them. On the other hand, you will notice that many people will be totally clear, balanced and unaffected at all. If you are in the latter group, you are on the right track. You may notice the change and the quickening, but you will be observing it from the outside. Those who feel like they are being churned are looking at it from the inside, and they are feeling the turmoil. In fact, as time speeds up, it will cause actual physical friction. People will notice themselves heating up when it is not hot. As you let go of the programs, patterns, illusions, false interpretations and beliefs, you will notice differences. There are many lessons to be learned about negotiating this new journey. As you align with the shifts and the transfiguration, you will notice it is smoother.

Making the Choice

We can liken this to an upward and downward spiral. During the period August, 1987 to January, 1993, you were in an open time, like being suspended in a large ball. You had freedom of choice for making decisions about what you were going to do in the future and how you were going to handle it. Many decided to choose no path and bumped along like a log in a river.

Toward the end of that period, you had to choose the upward or the downward spiral. You had to choose; there were no more time outs. Your choice set up and governed the direction you are in now. You still had time to change your direction until 1996, but with every passing day, moving from the downward spiral to the upward took more and more effort.

If you chose the upward spiral, you are flying; you made the right choice. But this is also where illusion can cause denial and misdirection. You may think you are flying, but it may be an illusion until you look down. If it is an illusion, you might crash.

Many people want to fly over their problems and their challenges, assuming that if they perform the right spiritual practices they can forget the past. Yes, you can forget the past, but that does not clear the past nor stop the lessons from continuing. The past is still there to remind you that it is the initial step on your spiritual path. Karmic lessons do not go away; they follow you from lifetime to lifetime.

The Akashic Record does not clear the lesson just because you want it to. You have to show that you've learned the lesson and know where you are on the path. The information is available; all you have to do is ask. Karmic contracts and agreements are just what they indicate. You cannot clear them unless you know what they are. When you become aware of the people with whom you have karmic contracts, you can release the person and the contract. Many people think that all they have to do is ask that the contracts be released and they are gone. But it doesn't happen like that. People claim to have released karmic contracts only to find that they've not even been addressed. Illusions work very well when you buy into the denial that accompanies them.

Those who had not made the decision by 1996 were shot out of the spiral, as were those in the downward spiral who resisted moving forward. Those of you who were ready to fly took off into the upward spiral in 1994 and are now finding it very easy. People who refused to take responsibility for their lives now find themselves in chaos, with challenges coming thick and fast.

You had nine years (1987 – 1996) to get your life in order. There is no time left to sit back and ask for time-outs. You have to take responsibility now. If you do not know what responsibility is, then you had better find out quickly. As time "quickens" or speeds up, you will have to make instant decisions. If you have gone through the door to rebirth, letting the past go and taking responsibility, it will be easy.

When you let go of the past, you have to forgive all the people in your past. Remember, *you* set up all of the situations in your life for them to harm you. Are you willing to release all the people in your past? Yesterday is history. All the situations that have happened to you in the past are in the past. Let them go. They are not supporting your future in a positive manner. The future can be positive, supportive, fun, and exciting. The framework is already set up. All you have to do is step onto the path. Are you ready to let go of your neediness and co-dependency to be wanted, your desire for outside validation? This is the first initiation.

Stepping onto the Path

To step onto the path, you must go through the second initiation. To go through this door, you must let your old self die and be reborn, but not in the way that a fundamentalist religionist would have you believe. Jesus Christ will not relieve you of the mistakes you have made in the past. He was sent to the Hebrews to show and teach them compassion, forgiveness, and love at a time when there was precious little of those qualities in their hearts. They did not get it then, and many of them still do not get it now. That is why the conflicts continue. They have been through seven tribulations to learn forgiveness, love, acceptance, and compassion. Karma keeps coming back on them but they do not seem to get it. They are in the eighth time around. Are they going to get it this time? Only time will tell. This is still a lesson-in-progress.

Jesus Christ said, "Forgive them, for they do not know what they are doing." He also said, "You can do anything I can do and many things better." These words are just as applicable today as they were then. Do you really believe that? If so, you have the ability to change the progression of the future on planet Earth. Most people have still not received the message today. Are you ready to take on the responsibility that the predicted Earth changes place before you? It is in your hands. You are totally responsible for the future. The current progression is changing because of many strong and willing souls who have assumed responsibility for spreading the word of love, compassion, and forgiveness.

Cosmic consciousness has already broken through into your reality. The critical mass was reached in 1996. When it was reached, a major separation happened as consciousness made a quantum leap forward.

Clearing the Conflicts

As you have seen, many conflicts, corruption, and contradictions which, in the past, were covered up are being exposed. People are demanding to know. Cover-ups will not be an option in the future. A small group of people are bringing this to the forefront as part of the program of consciousness shifts. All the conflicts of interest that are besieging the national and local politicians will come to the surface, with many resigning and many being convicted of fraud, etc. It affected the 1996 elections in the U.S. and tumultuous times will become the norm in the political arena. Those who are ethical and honest will survive. In fact, honesty and ethics will now be requirements to gain public office. This may be slower to come to critical mass because the general public will be the control factor in this action coming to fruition. The faster people wake up and take responsibility, the sooner it will happen. It may take a major conflict, such as Nixon and Watergate in the 1970s, for this to happen. Whitewater is the tip of an iceberg that will topple many political careers in both political parties and may even lead to a breakdown in your federal government. This is an open situation at this time and whether it comes to pass depends on how the people view the situation.

Because voters didn't wake up and take control of the direction of their government in 1996, Clinton was reelected. But he may not finish his second term, being forced to resign because of scandal and conflicts of interest. The final outcome of this episode is open to change depending on how the people respond to all the public disclosures of government conflict and corruption. Business has already begun to go through the same cleansing.

What caused the fall of Nixon and put many in jail for collusion seems to have been swept under the rug. It seems now that the Clinton administration has been involved in scandals, cover-ups and invading individual privacy to the point of being ludicrous. Nothing seems to be done about it. Congress has also had its share; what was considered treason 25 years ago is now commonplace. This will not continue and it may bring your government down.

The clearing is not only about the government and business; it is also about you, the general population. To enter the New Millennium, you have to clear your anger, fear, control, need for power, and manipulation. There will be no room for people who want someone to take care of them in the Aquarian Age. The new epoch is about cooperation, compassion, unconditional love, and forgiveness, but that does not mean it is an open door for freeloaders and people who want someone else to make their decisions for them. It is not about clinging to a group for security, either.

We want to stress that it's about reclaiming your power and personal responsibility. Taking your power back is difficult for many people. Taking responsibility for yourself requires you to let go of any neediness. Peace, happiness, harmony, and joy only happen when you carry your own load. That is the most important aspect of entering the New Millennium.

The Economic Climate

The reason we use the word *climate* is that it is heating up, not from inflation but from corruption. Your economy has been manipulated for the last 60 years. The phony oil crisis in the 1970s was a test of how people would react to a controlled economy. At that time, you bought it even though a few people tried to expose the cover-up. It won't happen again with oil.

The U.S. government tells you that the economy is in good shape but that simply is not true. It is being manipulated more than it ever has been in the past. In 1984, we saw a depression coming, and we predicted September 27, 1984, as the "Black Monday." It did not happen at that time because the Reagan administration intervened by supporting the silver market by buying up silver so the price did not plunge. As a result, the stock market experienced a minor correction and silver prices slid very slowly.

In 1987, the powers that run the financial world tried to force another break. It was stronger than in 1984 but it did not succeed either. The situation is different now; people are now stretched out on credit to the point that the credit ratio is about to break. There are over ten times more funds out on credit than there is money in circulation and it is reaching breaking point, yet people do not seem to recognize the situation. The Federal Government continues to print more money, put it into circulation and devalue your currency. Everyone is betting on the future.

There will be a point, as we see it, however, when you will no longer be able to hold it together and the whole financial market will crash. You are very close to that point now and the wizards of the financial field can bring it down any time they wish. If this wanton spending on credit does not stop, we see financial collapse as inevitable even if the wizards try to stop it. You can only sustain an economy up to a point. When the credit level reaches the point where the money in circulation will not pay the bills, then the system has to fall. With all the manipulation in the world money markets, we cannot predict a date for a collapse but it will come when credit exceeds the ability to repay debt. The coming changes will be all tied together if the chain reaction of greed does not cease.

Of course, there is another avenue, and it is being considered right now: to trigger rapid inflation by printing money wantonly, flooding the market, and devaluing the currency. If this happens, it will take a wheelbarrow of money to buy your basic needs, as happened in Germany. It could also happen in the U.S., and if it does, expect a world-wide depression before the year 2000. As in everything that is happening now, you are on the cusp of major change. That is why we are not predicting any specific outcome. It could change anytime, but we feel that it may take a financial collapse to wake people up. This means that your pensions and retirement funds will be worthless. Food will have more value than the dollar.

You have entered a time of rapid and tumultuous change at all levels of your existence. We recommend that to protect yourself from any panic in the near future, you pay off all your credit accounts. Begin to save some money in small bills such as $20 and smaller. If you can, buy junk silver coins—U.S. coins minted prior to 1964. You will pay the silver price for them. But there may be a time when they will have barter value when your paper money is worthless.

Begin to buy food products you can store without spoiling. However, don't rush to the store and buy thousands of dollars of food supplies. Buy a little extra each time you shop, especially grains which you can store in sealed containers. You can get gallon jars from restaurants or many places free or for a small cost.

It would be best to live outside the congested cities. Living in a place where you have some land to grow your own food would be ideal. We are aware that many cannot live in ideal conditions but you can begin to set up your situation so that it will be safer from a financial collapse.

Earth Changes

The Earth change predictions that you have known for the past 500 years are now being revised. You have opened the door to the possibility of a Golden Age with the onset of this New Millennium. The consciousness is now shifting to an upward spiral although it may not look that way from all the conflicts happening at this time. But enough people have lifted and evolved their basic awareness to a point that we are approaching critical mass. As we approach this point, you will be assisted by more highly developed societies from other galaxies.

As we said in the beginning of this dialogue, the projections we give here are merely probabilities, as they have not come to pass. You will notice that they are not in line with the Akashic Records, as we feel that the evolution of consciousness is moving at such an accelerating rate that the future is changing as fast as you think sometimes. It is very hard to make long range predictions because of the Quickening.

The retreat of the negative alien forces during 1996 was but one example. At the Intergalactic Council meeting, an agreement was reached with the Orion and Draco forces to pull back from any further attacks on planet Earth. The Sirians and Pleiadians called for action against Orions and Dracos if they did not pull back their forces. As a result, you only have to deal with the Dark Forces from your own Astral Plane now. They are a force to contend with because they do not want to see positive Earth changes. (Again, this prediction was not fulfilled in total until we took action. See "A Direct Discourse from the Intergalactic Council" near the end of this chapter.)

Many people ask us why someone would want to destroy the good things of this world. The answer requires the understanding that there are positive and negative forces to balance out every situation. During the creation of the universe, God created both positive and negative forces for balance in the universe. The negative got out of control with the same challenge that you are facing in this third-dimensional world—the greed for power and control. The Luciferian force gained power with all the fallen angels that fell into greed and bowed to that force.

Many people in body today work with and actually incarnated into negative forces. These forces work from a level that does not recognize the light of God or Christ because they have fallen so far down that they only see one way of getting control and that is to destroy. Many people are unwittingly working with, and are possessed by, these demonic Dark Forces and do not even know it.

You cannot see or perceive the demonic inter-dimensional entities, no matter how clairvoyant you are, because they slip between planes. Many souls are recruited by the Luciferian forces after they pass out of the body and become earthbound. They do not want to be dead, as they perceive it, and become caught up in the web of the Dark Forces. They get locked in that program and become programmed robots for the Dark Forces. They have infiltrated your government and that's why actions like Ruby Ridge and the Waco siege happened.

People who become possessed by these entities no longer have a conscience so they act almost like robots. They are driven by greed for power and control. If you try to step out of line, they want to destroy you because they feel you are a threat to their power. Many high government officials are controlled by these forces and will do anything, without fear of the consequences. They live in the present with no care for tomorrow, no fear about the future. The senseless killings and the fighting throughout your planet stem from the greed to control.

This is one of the main reasons that the Earth changes have precipitated as they have—the universal powers were waiting for you to wake up. We did not, and do not, want to destroy your planet, instead hoping that you would get the message sometime. Those on Atlantis did not get the message and you know what happened. We set up a progression that would culminate at the end of this epoch in the year 2000. You have now had plenty of time to wake up.

In your Bible, the writer John wrote about the end of time. The Book of Revelation is about this particular time in history. Read it and take heed. You may need an interpreter, as it is written in code but many teachers can interpret for you. You may also want to read the Psalms, as they are also about this time. Each one is for a year, from 1900 to 2050. They describe the effects of that year. Let us reiterate that we do not want to destroy your civilization. You will do that. You are given the tools and the teachings to follow; it is your choice.

Humanity does have one saving grace at this point. Many of you have heeded the warning and consciousness is almost to a point of shift, at critical mass. When that is reached, a major shift in the Quickening happens, and the dimensional shift begins to speed up. The Dark Forces will not be able to handle the vibrational shift and will lose their hold. People who are possessed by Dark Forces and cannot make this upshift will pass on and leave the planet. At this point, critical mass will occur and by 2002, the battle will be over.

Your main enemy now is your national governments and their Atlantean legacy of greed for power. The new world order is evidence of this action. As you have noticed, the disasters are hitting those areas where people are not waking up. As people wake up, the balance of power shifts toward them and governments will fall and crumble as corruption becomes public knowledge. Many governments rule their people by fear and anger. They will destroy themselves in time. The U.S. Government may do the same unless the greed for power and money is reversed.

The Atlantean greed for power was so intense and powerful that it caused a major earth shift only 8,500 years ago, which resulted in major Earth changes destroying their continent. That society, more technologically advanced than yours, destroyed itself with greed for power and control. This is the first time a major Earth change happened during an epoch—they usually transpire at the end of an epoch.

The Earth change maps that have been published predicted that you were headed on the same course but the Earth change progression has shifted and the old patterns will not happen. In fact, all the disasters will now be local and will befall only those people who are not aware of the requirements of the New Millennium.

Your Earth is a living being and responds well to love and compassion. And the shift in the coming Earth changes originates in those areas where these feelings predominate. The West Coast of the U.S. will not be destroyed as predicted in the past since it is now the spawning ground of the new consciousness. Many of the predicted earthquakes have been averted by the elevated consciousness on the West Coast of U.S.

Locations of the Earth Changes

As to locations of the Earth changes, we would redraw your map and place a large lake in the center of the U.S., instead of having the ocean taking over the western U.S. as many predict at this time. All of the following predictions can be modified as they have been in the past. Nothing is locked in place.

1. The St. Lawrence River will be blocked and will no longer exist because of a crustal uplift causing a major earthquake after the year 2000 on the Canadian border and in upstate New York southwest of Montreal. The coastal side will become a salt water bay.

2. The result of this shift will be that the flow of all of the major rivers from the northern states that feed the Great Lakes will be feeding south into the Mississippi River, flooding the low-lying areas permanently where they were flooded in 1993–94. More extensive flooding will produce a major lake in the states south of Lake Michigan which will put much farmland under water.

3. The Midwest will experience major flooding as the rivers create new watercourses feeding into the new lake along the Mississippi River. These areas will be free of earthquakes. Severe weather patterns will spawn tornadoes.

4. Areas along the East Coast will experience heavy tidal wave action from these earth upheavals. It would be best to be at least 150 miles inland from the coast.

5. Washington, D.C., the new Babylon, will be totally destroyed by earthquakes, floods and fires.

6. Areas off the coast of Florida will rise to the surface, bringing parts of the old Atlantean continent to the surface again. It has been slowly rising over the last 200 years. People will begin to skin dive in the area to investigate the shallow waters that were unreachable 60 years ago.

7. The Gulf Coast will be flooded as the level of the Gulf of Mexico rises from the flooding Midwestern rivers. It will extend into Texas and Louisiana up to 200 miles from the coast.

8. Due to a series of increasingly intense earthquakes, the Wasatch Fault from Canada to south of Salt Lake City will activate, causing all the water in Salt Lake to disappear.
9. Areas of the Southwest will see very little activity.
10. The West Coast will experience many strong offshore earthquakes, causing large tidal waves that will inundate coastal cities. If the consciousness continues to elevate, it will moderate the intensity. Many areas along the coast will experience extensive damage from tidal waves caused by the earthquakes. This will cause flooding inland to Sacramento. The coastal area will be flooded, both north and south. A major split will form along the San Andreas fault line. The areas of the coastal plains which have been built on landfill will turn to consistency of quicksand and buildings will sink. However, California and the western states will *not* sink and fall into the ocean or disappear. Most of the earthquakes will center in the large cities on both coasts where greed for power and control exists. San Francisco and Los Angeles will experience major destruction, but will not be destroyed completely.
11. Many of the inactive volcanoes will erupt along the Ring of Fire along the West Coast, Japan, and the South Pacific region, causing tidal waves from the shock waves.
12. At this point, Japan appears very unstable and will experience major damage from earthquakes and flooding.
13. The Northwestern states will experience some earthquakes. The major danger is the inactive volcanoes and flooding.
14. The pole shift is scheduled to take place on May 5, 2000, as the planets align as they did 6,500 years ago. Depending on the severity of the pole shift, the ice caps on the poles may slip into the ocean. If they do, sea level will raise by up to 400 feet. *We must emphasize that this may not happen.*

The poles will not make a major shift as predicted in the past. As of 1998, your planet's magnetic north is almost 20 degrees off true north and the strength of its magnetic field has been dropping for many years. The adjustment will bring the magnetic field back to true north. At this time, the North Pole will shift down toward Russia. The South Pole will shift up toward southern Chile. As a result, the equator will realign. The severity of the shift is controlled by the consciousness of the people on your planet. It may just be a realignment and will be about 21 or 22 Degrees.

Everything is fluid at this time. Your shift in consciousness controls the outcome. Planet Earth is a living being and will respond to love and support in cleaning up the environment. The whole shift process is intended to rid the planet of those who are destroying it.

Another phenomenon to discuss is the Photon Belt, a highly-charged particle field with no precedence in your science. Some people predict that it heralds three days of total darkness but that is not going to happen. It will, however, cause a period of darkness when you get into the dense center, similar to an eclipse of the sun. It will affect electricity for a short time, but will not disrupt communication for a long period. As of 1996, you were on the fringes of the belt, which is why weather patterns began to be so erratic at that time, but consciousness can also mitigate the effect of the Photon Belt.

These are general readings and are only good for the time given. Each day can, and, will change the outcome as you move toward a quantum jump in time and the quickening accelerates. Increasing numbers of aware people will moderate the effect as we have already seen. The biggest detriment to moderating the changes is fear of them or apathy toward them.

Who Is Your Source?

When you tune into a source, the Akashic Records, or the collective unconscious data bank, you get what you are asking or looking for. Also remember that the Dark Forces can work against you when you are not clear. If possessive spirit beings are attached to you, they can subvert the message coming to you. They can also directly channel to you, masquerading as a spirit guide. If you are not sure as to the identity of your source, you may be tuned into a spirit guide from the dark side.

Recently, the Orions and Dracos, who considered Earth a garden planet, launched an intense effort to take control. They are now out of the picture, but astral beings with demonic overshadows are still on the scene now. They are less powerful than the aliens but they can and do cause considerable problems. They would like to see the historical Earth changes continue as predicted. They prefer to work through people who do any form of counseling or therapeutic work involving people since this allows them to control people without their knowledge. They will help healers create miracles so they can draw a larger numbers of people to them. So, it behooves anyone delivering any form of prophesy to be very clear who the source is.

The prophesy in the Bible is a good example of what has happened in the past. The Hebrews viewed God as a vengeful God who would take them to task. Many of the current fundamentalist religions interpret the Bible directly and live in the same fear. This is totally opposite to God's view. The view of God is, "all people are forgiven, no matter what they may have done." God has no negative reference point from which to judge anyone. You are the one who judges yourself.

All karma is self-created and self-imposed, although you may have invited many people to play into your lesson. If so, it is their lesson, too. Karma is a double-edged sword. Both people can learn the lesson, or both can be hurt by the lesson. Conversely, one can learn the lesson without the help of the other person. It is your choice all the way. All you have to do is claim Grace, and you can be relieved of your karma once you learn the lesson.

We have sent humanity many great teachers through the ages, in hopes that you would listen. And humanity seems to start over with a good, fresh outlook, but it always deteriorates and falls back into the same old ways of greed, control, authority, conflict, manipulation, and seeking power over others. This time we decided to send you many more teachers who could work more closely with individuals.

We choose the teachers and many are guided by us in their work. But, this also allows self-proclaimed teachers, shamans, gurus, and medicine people to claim to be connected with us. *Many may even claim to be ascended beings who have come back to teach.* They do not have the true Source as their guide. So please use your discernment to pick the pearls from the garbage. But even the charlatans may have one or two pearls for you. You must decide who is giving you the clear picture.

From our vantage point, we see many who do not recognize their ability to become teachers, and we challenge you, "Are you willing to stand up and be counted?" Those who have stepped forward are making the difference. As a result of your efforts, the future is not locked in, as it was in the past.

We also admonish you not to fall back on your laurels and feel you have done your part. The New Millennium requires you to be eternally vigilant. Keep yourself in a bubble of love and forgiveness. Be compassionate, but don't get empathetic and jump into other people's problems. Granted, there is pain and suffering on your planet, but that doesn't mean you have to suffer with them. Be compassionate and detached. Do not let your ego take over and get into a place where it is pumping you up, otherwise you may have to eat humble pie. Your main challenge is to overcome the illusions and the denials that all people suffer from. Separation from self is the most common condition of humanity. Take your power back and step into your power. Let go of the fear and speak your truth.

Thank you for listening,

— **The Source**

Discourse with the Intergalactic Council

When the Source feels I would get better information and results, they will act as a telephone operator and connect me up with another source of information as they have done in the following transmissions. I feel this is a very important link in my communication, because I am able to go through the astral Fourth Dimension with the help of my Higher Self, the Holy Spirit, the Presence of God and My Guardian Angel. By using Source as guide and telephone operator, this link blocks out any Dark Forces who want to break in and communicate through me. I can be guaranteed that the source I am talking with is a supportive group.

The Intergalactic Council is made up of five members from each star or planet group. Planet Earth is entitled to representation, but her people do not recognize the extraterrestrial connection at this time. There are people who are aware of the connection but refuse to acknowledge it. We could have more say in our destiny if we did have representation.

I opened by discussing the recent problems with the Orions. There seem to be some rebellious Orions implanting people with demonic beings. I asked if they would check this out and stop it.

From the Intergalactic Council,

We thank you for contacting us in relation to the continued intervention and incursion by the Draco forces on your planet Earth. We have taken action to stop their connection with the forces from your Astral Plane. As to the rebellious Orions, in every society there are the wayward types who refuse to follow the rules and laws given to govern and provide a reasonable way of life. You have them on your planet, too.

The criminal element exists throughout the universe. The reason they are reacting so maliciously is that they are aware that their days are numbered. They are trying to get a foothold, hoping that they can continue their unethical ways and continue to exist in the New Millennium. They do not want the change. They live in an illusion that life will continue the same. All they have to do is move with the change, but it will not happen. We cannot control that faction, short of pursuing them and tracking them down. With this information out, they may back off.

The dimensional shift and the dawn of the New Millennium is occurring not just in your galaxy but throughout the universe. Moving toward this fifth-dimensional shift will literally eliminate the criminal element from our universe. Beings of lower vibration will not be able to survive the shift. It will create too much friction within the aspects of themselves to function. Of course, their souls will not be destroyed, but they will have to return to the spiritual plane to reevaluate their past and deal with the karma they have created.

Every soul has toyed with or entered the dark side at one time in its existence. Life has existed in this universe for 40 million years and average soul involvement with the physical plane has been about 450,000 years. So you can assume that at some time the enticement of power and control has drawn most souls to the dark side to experience that form of life. You will have to clear this aspect of yourself. Over the next few years, your dark side will come up for you to face and clear.

You will not enter the New Millennium without clearing all your karma. The new universe will not tolerate illusion or dishonest behavior. This does not mean just in your relations with others. It means that you have to be totally honest with yourself. Any and all claims you make must be verifiable with your teachers on the Inner Planes. Many have, in the past, acted or masqueraded as spirit guides, master teachers, and ascended masters. Please use your discernment at its highest level to find out if you are being misled. It is your responsibility if you get on the wrong track and find yourself back in the cycle of return (reincarnation).

Nobody will warn you if you only *think* you have the truth. You probably wouldn't listen anyway, since you have the truth.

Being that you are willing to be controlled by your illusions and discarnate beings, they will invalidate any other information also. Your teacher will not intervene and say, "You are listening to the wrong source. You'd better wake up."

You may wake up to find yourself on an unexpected trip. You may think it is ascension, but you may find yourself with many friends who have the same disillusional beliefs that they are on the right track, only to find out that they are still on the reincarnational wheel. The merry-go-round of the cycle of return starts again. Maybe you will be a little more discerning in who you listen to on your next trip into a body. We find it interesting that so many people on your plane of existence are willing to listen to any voice outside of your physical realm. Most people do not even check the credentials of their sources. Use discernment before you accept direction and advice from beyond your own awareness.

On our plane of existence, everything operates from integrity, ethics and honesty, even in war. When a commitment is made, it is adhered to. In a December, 1996 meeting, according to your calendar, we discussed the Draco and Orion action on your planet. They were told to pull back their forces, and they did so. It is our understanding that you have had no further problems with them until you discovered this incident that you brought to our attention. Right? (The channel affirms.)

We have now discovered that the Draco's contact with your planet caused them to fall into your behavior patterns. They assumed that they could get away with dishonest, unethical actions because this is the way on your planet. We know that you will rise above this pattern in the coming shift, so we are not criticizing, just observing. Now that we have recognized this behavior, it will cease.

We did not see the need to check on them because it is not how our society operates. The accepted norm is that you do what you say will do and that is accepted without going back to check. We do not have to be continually on guard. It is a good way to be, since there is no security problem. You will rise above that behavior during the coming New Millennium shift.

The earlier question you asked about our planned intervention, such as making an announcement over your radio and TV stations has been put off. We have delayed it due to the fact that we would be considered pirates, or intruders, and our message would not be believed.

With your fear of aliens and your warlike behavior toward them, we would have to defend ourselves from attack. We do not respond in that manner. As soon as enough people will listen to what we have to say and support our visit, we will make that announcement.

We see massive changes coming in your system as the influence of honesty and clarity begins to take effect. It is already happening as people become aware of the corruption in your system of values. When a society is headed for change, drastic action has to be taken to correct the misdirection. The reaction to this is all the fighting and the crime that stems from fear from loss of control and power. It will get worse at local levels. We do not see a worldwide battle or war, but local insurrections and civil wars. You could have one in your country if the present corruption continues.

If you are interested in the future of your planet, you will adhere to the principles of Love, Forgiveness, Compassion, and Acceptance. Letting go of judgment is your main lesson. The "top dog-underdog" routine has been in force on your planet for many thousands of years.

The battle for control of people has been a paramount desire in men's minds. Not only do they not understand what peace is but most have lost even the concept of peace. It is now coming back, and is on the rise, as people are now talking who refused to do so in the past. Many times, it may be just coexistence, but it is a step in the right direction. As we see it, you are headed for much better times once you pull out of the basic corruption and grapple for power.

Thank you for informing us about the Draco/Orion situation.

Transmission Two

To the InterGalactic Council:

We have had a major conflict with the Orions. They won't let up at all. They continue to attack relentlessly, with implants and cords. They are using demonic inter-dimensional entities to do their dirty work. When I was hit by the demonic guards trying to enforce a past life curse and hex, we decided we had to get to the bottom of the control mechanism they were using. As we searched for the implant, door, or gate, they were getting through, we discovered a tracking implant that was wired up to my pituitary, pineal and hypothalamus. With further research, we found a modem that was wired to my neurological system and my ears.

My hearing had been slowly going down until I could hardly hear anything. When we removed these implants, my hearing started to return. When we removed the curses and hexes, we found a karmic guard that was trying to control implants. We asked for the solution to the situation, and, before we could communicate with you, we had the problem solved.

We discovered that the Orions were tracking people by computer with the tracking implant. Not only that, but I was one of the 12 computer engineers who were able to get into the Akashic Records and I had the access code to Orion computers. This was done over 12,000 years ago. In this manner, they have access to all Akashic Records; they know all about a person and can track them. I was able to go back to the records and get the access code to the Orion computers.

When I gave the access code to the Higher Selves and the Brotherhood of Light, I asked them to put a virus in, or jam, the Orion computers. Immediately, the Orions shut their computers down. We have not heard from, nor have we had any contact with them since August 26, 1996. What happened to them, and did we actually cause them to leave the planet?

From the InterGalactic Council:

Yes, you did the right thing; in fact, you were the only person who could have accomplished the mission you just finished. All the other members of your team who broke into the Akashic Records continue to align with rebellious Pleiadians and the Orions. In fact, you have created quite a rumble in the ranks. That is why they were hitting you so hard. They wanted to take you out before you could accomplish what you did. You broke their communication link with the Dark Forces. Now that we have the access code, they are not likely to use their computers in the way they had been.

When you look at the feat you accomplished single-handed, it is amazing you survived their onslaught. Do you realize the value of the task you accomplished? This was major service to your planet. It is clear sailing from here because all the alien forces are pulling out. This opens the door for the supportive groups to take charge and help you out.

Remember, even though the Orions have left, we are not going to make a landing until we know we will be supported in our effort to help you. At the present time, your government is describing us as alien intruders, with no differentiation between criminal and supportive aliens. Under cover, they know that we are not intruders but to cover up all their covert activities, they have to play their present role out so that the population will not catch on to their agenda.

We have worked with your planet's governments since 1954 but everything has been covered up so that all the "black projects" financed by your governments will be kept in secret. The Dark Forces moved in during the 1960s and have been in power up to the present. Since you have forced Orions and the Dracos to leave your planet, things may change now.

Too many people on your planet are in illusion. Everything is not light and love. It is plain hard work to pull your planet out of the doldrums. You are on the brink of destruction, yet many people do not even realize it. We want to share our knowledge and technology with you, but we have found out that your governments want to use it for control and power plays.

The new world order's program has been around for over 12,000 years on your planet. Each group gets to the brink of taking total control, and they are destroyed with their culture and society. Are you ready to start over, stripped of all your advancements to this point? Each time, your society has taken a step back in technology when you have to start over.

We tried to establish a viable society on your planet 28,000 years ago. We left when Atlantis was destroyed. We left you a legacy of information in our pyramids and other buildings we constructed when we left. You will not be able to get access to this information until your governments stop their quest for the new world order, with the greed for control and power. These battles have been going on for millions of years.

Each planet, or star system, goes through an evolutionary unfolding before human life forms can exist on it. Your planet is relatively young on the evolving scale of the galaxy.

Many thousands of years ago, Mars was in the same position your planet is currently in. The same type of people, with the same consciousness of greed for power and control who took control of Mars, are now trying to take over your planet. Mars was rendered uninhabitable and you are headed for the same destiny.

We have an outpost laboratory and settlement on Mars but we are not going to let your cameras or Mars probes take pictures of our outpost. That is why the Mars mission satellites and probes are disabled before they can take pictures. Your governments know this because we have communicated with them. This is all part of the cover-up so you will buy their propaganda. They know they are wasting money, but they will continue to play the cover-up game, even though they know the facts.

Your only saving grace is that there is a committed group of souls on your planet who are waking up to the reality that they can change the course of events. We applaud their work and discipline but it will take real commitment to move into the place where you can actually step out of the illusion and into reality.

Many individuals who have started out with the right intention have lost their center and let their ego take control. This has allowed them to be taken over by Dark Forces. The shift was so subtle that they did not recognize the change in source of their information. It is not obvious to their audience, either. It is an insidious move by the Orions to instruct the astral beings on how to take over individuals or an organization.

When they get control, very few will recognize it. Their objective is to take control through insidious methods and hope the person does not recognize the attachment. In this way, they can move in and slowly take control, using these public figures as mouthpieces. If you listen closely and accurately, you can detect the message by the language and the manner it is delivered.

Most people do not want to recognize that the activity of the Dark Forces is affecting them. You can see this by their response when someone offers to clear them. They never have the time or the willingness to involve themselves in clearing of implants, cords, or attached Dark Forces. They are always the speaker, therapist or teacher. Very seldom, if ever, do they allow others to work on them.

This is exactly what the Dark Forces want because, with the exit of the Dracos and the Orions, they do not have the technology to operate as they have in the past.

Quite often, when the Dark Forces take over, they will make claims which will not come to pass because the Dark Forces are bent on creating fear. They would also like to get people to give over their power to some guru or teacher who will guide them through the darkness of the future. These misdirected individuals are akin to the Anti-Christ who will lead people astray and not prepare them for the coming changes. All the true Christ-centered teachers will tell you they cannot guide you through the darkness, but they can give you the tools and direction to light the way. You have to tread the path yourself. Nobody is going to carry you over the mountain and come to rescue you in a space ship and take you away to paradise.

You are already in paradise. Earth is the "garden planet." This why the aliens want to take it over. Protect it and take care of it, be a world server and deliver your planet into the New Millennium. The critical mass is coming to a crest now. You are ones who cause and create your heaven or hell.

The Dark Forces are losing their hold, thanks to a few individuals who are willing to stand up to themselves and defend your planet. It takes a considerable amount of courage to stand up to an invisible enemy when you being attacked by them. This is all coming to an end. There are teachers in your midst that show you how to protect yourself.

The reason we are not concerned with the criminal types is that we know that they cannot survive the shift in physical form. They will return to the spiritual world as will many on your planet. They have been given a clear opportunity to see the New Millennium and what can be expected. Many beings on our level of existence have fallen way below their level of competence and will no longer be allowed to continue their war-like behavior. They know the rules of the game and will be required to adhere to them. If they cannot do so, then they will revert to a lower level of existence on a work planet before they can move back to our level. You cannot violate Universal Law and continue to live in the New Millennium.

We realize that you have been hit by everything that has been able to hit your planet in the past. But it is humanity that allowed your planet to drop to a very low level of existence which left you vulnerable to attack and takeover. Being on your planet is contagious to beings who have not previously been exposed to unethical criminal behavior. When they see that it works, they are drawn into the web of greed for power and control. The temptation to use your abilities in a negative way is very hard to resist when you have the knowledge and technology we have. When you are exposed to the opportunity, it becomes easy to fall away from the truth. You were all at our level many millennia ago, but you chose to fall away, and the further you fell, the less you understood who you were. You are being given an opportunity to clear the path so you can step into the New Millennium now. The challenge you have is to follow the proper path.

There are many deceivers on your planet now, mainly your own people, living in illusion and denying their own truth. They conduct workshops, seminars, and conferences, telling you the way. Be very careful and use your discernment. Many of them are directly controlled by the Dark Forces and don't even know it. In fact, they will deny it and justify their work as being in the Christ Light. The only beings that can evaluate your work are from the Brotherhood of the Light. They are our teachers, too. We do not claim to be the ultimate authority. We have achieved light bodies, but that does not mean we are the authority. We still have lessons to learn, too.

As we said before, we cannot intervene in your affairs. We can provide help, but you have to pull yourself up to our level. When we see that you will support us in landing on your planet, we will. Many of our ancestors left your planet because it was sinking to low levels of consciousness. We have no need to fight anyone, or to defend anything. When people on your planet understand that concept, they will learn to live in peace. It is beginning to happen now.

Take a stand and get behind those who are taking their position to clear the planet. Do not let fear drive you back. Get out of auto-pilot and recognize your power. It will take action to rescue your planet. Meditation will help raise the vibration of the planet, but it will take action on your part to reach the critical mass that is required to make the transition into the New Millennium. It is your choice.

Remember, your planet is a spoke in the wheel. If you blow your planet out, it will throw the whole galaxy out of balance. The New Millennium is a major shift in the whole Universe. The coming fifth-dimensional shift will clear the whole Universe of negativity. This why the Dark Forces are working so hard to stop the shift. They know they cannot survive the high frequency of the shift.

Please support yourself so we can support you.

Live in peace.

Transmission Three

To the Intergalactic Council,

It was very upsetting to realize that our short-lived peace and harmony was again disrupted by Andromedans. I had never suspected that they would fall into the trap of manipulating another's freedom. All I have ever heard was they were here to help and support. Obviously, as their people have told me, criminals exist in every society. So what do we do? They seem to have taken over the Pleiadian role. Have they been around for a long time just observing? And why are they moving in now?

These alien forces are much more technologically advanced. There seems to be no way we can protect ourselves from them. They can set up programs in our body that will cause disease, illness, and neurological dysfunction. Fortunately I have a process to release, destroy and remove these programs. What about the people who have no knowledge of their tactics? What happens to people who are victims of their attacks and blame it on something physical? We are in a quandary. What do we do?

From the Intergalactic Council:

We understand your frustration, but there is little we can do to help you. There are criminal elements in every society as we have told you before. You are dealing with one of the most advanced races in the universe. Unfortunately they are using their power in a negative manner. You will have to wait until they lose their power or become aware that they are about to revert to lower dimensional beings and return to their home planet. When they do, they will be treated as criminals and disciplined as such. The Pleiadians met with the same treatment when they returned home. It is true that they are violating Universal Law but there is no police agency that will stop them.

To the Intergalactic Council:

What about the power and presence of God? Nobody should have to suffer these attacks without some protection.

From the Intergalactic Council:

We will answer with some history, since you do not seem get the basic understanding of why you are being treated as you are. In the beginning of time, everything was balanced and in order. As time progressed, there were those societies that advanced and did not go through the great fall. They evolved and rose to higher levels. However, many declined as did yours. They devolved and lost their direction.

Your planet was almost destroyed many times before, to cleanse it of the negativity, and it may have to undergo the same experience again before it can make this dimensional shift. No negative forces will be carried into the new millennium with the evolution of your planet. When you stand out like a beacon of degradation, of power that is out of control, you attract all the negative elements and dark forces of the universe, as have you. It is like a sewage plant of the Universe where all the garbage is cleansed and recycled, ready to be returned and reused.

You cannot destroy matter. Nor can you destroy a soul, but you can really foul it up and degrade it until it is nonfunctional and must be cleaned up. The question should be: *Can you redeem yourselves? Are you ready for salvation, as your religions state?*

The power of God is always present in your life. The question is: *Can you recognize it?*

You have been told many times before that there are no victims, but only people who choose to be victimized. When you live in a sewer, you have to climb out and rise to the level of evolution you seek. You have been telling people to take responsibility and reclaim their personal power for many years. Are they doing it? The power of God is always here. But God *never* intervenes. *God is Forgiveness and Acceptance. That is what you must learn.*

As your Bible states: "God helps those who help themselves." As you attune yourselves to the higher consciousness you are, to the presence of God within, you are protected. *This power cannot manifest within you as long as you deny your own power.* In other words, you must take control of your life and be a self-actualized being.

You have been teaching this for years, but most people give it only lip service, such as, "I know. I'm working on it." They do not really hear you in the depth of their being. Enlightenment and ascension are buzz words in your culture. Very few people really understand the concepts of ascension or enlightenment, let alone practice even the basic steps. This is why your planet is at the point it is in its own evolution. Granted, there is a large movement toward enlightenment, but that movement must focus on those processes that work. Most of the practices people on your planet use are symptomatic, or work only on the surface, never getting down to the real cause of disruption of your people.

Liken this to an animal that senses fear in a person. The animal will not attack people who are strong and have a sense of their personal power, but will attack a person who is in fear. This is a rule of the universe to eliminate the weak species. It may seem callous, but your society has weakened itself by protecting the weak and trying to support those who don't want to take responsibility. Granted there exceptions to this, but the victims will be your downfall. As they proliferate, they will become a moving force on your planet since they will elect leaders who will support their needs.

Taking responsibility is foreign to the victims of a society. They see themselves as being taken advantage of by that society, so they are entitled to welfare, etc. At the other end are the people who control your businesses and who take advantage of these people. Then you have the bureaucrats and the politicians who play to the "poor me" victims. Your whole form of government and societal rules are out of control. So why are you surprised that the negative forces are attracted to your planet? Does that answer your questions?

The Pleiadian and Andromedan forces did not know how to function as negative dark forces until they were introduced to the role on your planet. Some were attracted to the abuse of power and control, and the manipulation they observed. Others saw people who were victims and out of control, giving their power away. They saw it as game at first. Then they realized they could actually use their abilities to move in and take control of governments and businesses, too. This was their fall from grace. The desire to wield power got out of control and began to control them. As a result, they now manipulate the majority of your businesses and governments. That's why you see so much white collar crime and so much disregard for ethics and integrity in your government. These aliens are like fallen angels who lost sight of their power and are now using it in violation of universal law. It does not make any difference where you are in your evolution. You can fall when you lose sight of the goal.

The Dracos and the Orions recognized this when they were told to pull back. At this point, the Andromedans have not yet recognized their mistake. We cannot predict what they will do. The Pleiadians recognized it in time and retreated, almost losing their positions. But, they had to pay the price for their indiscretion when they arrived back home.

We can see what is happening but we will not step in to help you at this time unless you recognize your own situation and begin to pull yourself out of the hole into which you have fallen. You have dishonest, unethical governments with politicians who seem to think they can get away with just about anything. You have people who are fighting age-old battles for the elusive power of control. You have nations who have fought religious wars for centuries. Where is the love and forgiveness that the major teachers of this last millennium were teaching? When is your planet's population going to recognize that you do not have much time left to make a decision? Time is running out, and there are no more time-outs left in the game. You must make your decision now!

To the Intergalactic Council,

I made my decision a long time ago. How do I get others to follow through with their commitments? This still does not answer all my questions? I know why I'm being targeted, but if I take responsibility to do what I can to support the evolution of this planet, why do I get no protection?

From the Intergalactic Council,

In this case we will refer you to the Sirian Command. They may have an answer to your dilemma.

From the Sirian Command,

As the Council told you, there are criminal elements in the Universe. We do not have an intergalactic police force, nor are we willing to track down rebel forces. We control our own people and that is where we draw the line.

Even though we are aware that you were once one of our people, you departed our society many thousands of years ago. You fell into the very situation about which you now complain. In fact, you were a very powerful person in the dark forces for many years. We see that you have recovered your path and are on your journey toward enlightenment and ascension, but that does not enable us to protect you. You still have bridges to cross. We can protect you at times but we are not your guardian angels. We will send a group to support you when the going gets especially tough. We will track your progress and support you when you have serious attacks. Fortunately, when the Andromedans lose their power, it does not look as if any alien groups will take their place.

As we have said before, we cannot move in and help you until your government accepts us as friendly supporters. As long as the rebel aliens control your government, we will not intervene. Again, it is a matter of personal responsibility and integrity versus control, power, and manipulation. At this point, the rebels do not want you to know we exist. Your people are falling for that line at this time. As you move toward the New Millennium, things will change and we will reconsider our decision.

The main problem seems to be that your people are unwilling to recognize the gravity of the situation. They are operating on automatic pilot, as if there was nothing "out of synch" on your planet. But many governments and economies are on the verge of collapse. Note all the investigations going on into practices in the U.S. government. We do not have to list the situations on your planet at its lowest point on the scale of evolution. Your people are operating as if to have a roof over their head, money in their pocket, and a job is reality. They are living in delusion, avoiding the truth of reality. The U.S. government falsifies facts and figures to make your controlled and manipulated economy look good, but it is still on a rapid downhill slide.

So what is the conclusion? Your saving grace is the fact that this millennium is coming to a close and your planet is soon going to cleanse itself. How devastating that will be is up to you. Your population has to take personal responsibility and become ethical in their dealings with each other and tell the truth. All the denial, blame, and illusion has to be overcome one way or another or you will be forced into doing it.

Also, those working toward enlightenment should reevaluate their path and their programs. Overall, some people have made major progress, but most have not. Most are just scratching the surface. The programs need more depth.

The positive aspect is that you are powerless to hold the planet back from its transformation to the fifth dimension. It will go through that transfiguration with or without your help. The only question is, how many will survive the shift? The ball is in your court now. Only a few years remain.

Good luck on your journey to enlightenment. We know you will make the grade. How many will you bring with you?

Transmission Four

To the Intergalactic Council:

On a recent Art Bell show, I heard Col. Philip Corso discuss the Roswell incident (the UFO that crashed at Roswell, NM in July 1947). He contended that all the new inventions that have surfaced in the last 40 years have been seeded by ETs into various corporations. He listed such advances as night vision equipment, lasers, fiber optics, integrated circuits, Kevlar plastic armor, particle beam devices that became a reality in just a few short years. He claimed that all this information, which was seeded into Hughes Aircraft, IBM, Bell Labs, and Dow Corning without their knowledge, were the precursors to the new equipment that is being built today.

Curso also claimed that ETs used thought control devices to direct their saucers because they move at such a rate of speed that manual control would be impossible. And now aircraft manufacturers are working on mind-directed devices to control aircraft since they are attaining speeds where manual control is too slow to effectively and safely handle aircraft.

Curso's claims seem plausible considering how many years it took us to develop machinery in the past. He makes many other claims in his book, *The Day After Roswell,* but I am more interested in how we developed such amazing devices in less than 35 years.

Many reviewers try to debunk the book as science fiction, imagination, or just another novel poking in the dark about UFOs. What is the truth in this? Are the ETs that were recovered from this wreck and others real? What is their origin? The aliens I have been dealing with are light beings. If your people manifested a body, would they actually look like this? Are they automatons ? Do they function as robots? Was the information actually seeded into scientists' minds as Corso contends?

From the Sirian Command:

You are asking highly technical questions that may cause a stir in official circles. We can give you the answers but we warn you that you will be debunked just like Corso was. The cover-up in your political and scientific circles to block the truth is ludicrous and the only reason we can think of is loss of control if people were to know the truth.

In answer to your questions, yes, we do use thought to control our vehicles. We actually become one with the vehicle such that it responds to our thought, allowing us to make instant course adjustments. Your people know all about this guidance process. In fact, you have already developed a similar guidance process for your aircraft, and yes, these beings are automatons, clones developed for space travel that function as robots. It was a way for us to impart our knowledge to you in a way that could be accepted.

As far as transferring information to your scientists, we had to set up a mind control process so that they felt that they controlled the program. We did send some people in to give you the information but your Government hit men killed them because they would not cooperate in the cover-up. Two of them were Nikola Tesla and Royal Lee. Those alive now are afraid to go public with what they know. One in your midst now is David Adair. He is willing to reveal much of what he knows so we are protecting him and will continue to do so.

We are light beings and we do not need physical bodies to function. No, we would not appear like our automatons. If we want to do so, we can appear in bodies similar to yours but we choose not to do so. We can and do use mind control in many ways as you have seen when we transfer information to your scientists but, at this time, we choose not to do so. The rebel aliens are using mind control now in a negative manner to manipulate people in your government, military, and business. When people operate on "autopilot," it is very easy for the rebels to step in and take control. If you would only wake up and take personal responsibility to move your frequency up, they would not be able to affect you.

Have a great trip on your journey in enlightenment.

To the Sirian Command:

That sounds great but the challenge is keeping calm so that we do not get upset and open a door to them. We have become aware that every time we allow ourselves to go out of balance by getting into fear, anger, justification or compromising ourselves, we get hit by Andromedans, They are watching us at all times, waiting for us to slip or fall so they can move in and take control. As far as I can see, there is no way we can protect ourselves at all times. Clearing all the programs that block us from enlightenment takes time. It seems that most people are not willing to spend the time or money to achieve that goal. So where are we in this dilemma?

To the Source of My Being:

I am open to whomever you wish to direct this question.

From the Source:

We will take the question, but we warn you this may not be the answer you want. Saviors never survive the battle, so don't put yourself in that position. You can only help those who want to help themselves. Heard that before? You can only set an example. If people do not want to follow your path, that is up to them. We can give you answers, but that does not mean people will listen.

Those who have eyes to see and ears to hear will understand the message. Those who do not want to hear or follow the direction of the message may kill the messenger. Do not become a martyr. Everyone chooses his or her path, so do not try to save people unless they ask for help. This is the downfall of your society.

"The meek shall inherit the earth" does not mean that the victims who back away from confrontation, those who are in denial of the truth, and the down-trodden are the chosen ones. The meaning is: "those who choose to take responsibility, to take the path of forgiveness and acceptance with no need for control and authority will be the survivors of the coming earth changes."

Remember the phrase in *A Course in Miracles:* "All are called; few choose to listen." That was changed by the Roman Catholic Church to read "Many are called; few are chosen." This is a good example of the mind control that has existed for over 1,600 years. The bible was rewritten at the conference of Nicea in 325 AD by the Pope and Cardinals to read in this manner so they could control the people. How many people want an intermediary to talk for them? We are here to communicate with anyone who chooses to listen.

You are on the right path in your process to clear all the emotional blocks and childhood trauma. Your vibrational level increases every time you remove a program that holds you back from ascension. Your method of closing the doors and gates will also provide the protection you desire.

The path is clear and the door is open. Continue on your way.

— **The Source**

4

Who and Where Are You?

PROBABLY THE DEEPEST AND MOST often asked questions are: "Who am I? Why am I? Where am I? Where am I going?" You can engage in a lifetime of introspection and come up with many answers. But are they the right answers? We can practice all the proper techniques and take all the appropriate steps which we think will lead us to the evolution of our soul. The only glitch is: is it an illusion or is it reality?

We all want to think we are taking the right path, yet I find many people in denial of who they really are. We are a result of our past lives and the lessons we have not cleared or finished. And we carry the latter forward to each future life. We start out at the same place where we left off in our past life. Neuro/Cellular Repatternning (N/CR) gives the opportunity to open the files from all our past lives and clear them by claiming Grace. Through the process of clearing used in N/CR, we can clear as many as 25 to 50 lifetimes in one session. (See Appendix C for more information about N/CR.)

It is important to know the way your mother felt about her nine-month trip in bringing you into the world, how your father responded to you entering the family, if you were the gender they desired, and how you were accepted by any siblings. This opened the first chapter of your life and set up your current life program. How you were treated after you were born opened the second chapter of your present life programs. How you responded or reacted to them opened the third chapter and set the stage for the play of your life. Your parents did not choose you. You set this up before you made the choice of your family. The rest is history. How you reacted to your treatment by your primary caregivers set up the program of your life.

Growing up, you may have felt you were in the back seat most of the time but you had it all programmed by the time you were three years old.

Many of us were told we had to be "seen and not heard," so we closed down. Too many times we felt rejected and began to make interpretations about who we were, mostly that we were not all right because of the way we were treated. If negative feelings kept coming up, we began to reject ourselves. The self-talk started to take over and we sold out to our ego and its sub-personalities. They began to run our lives. They did a reasonable job of protecting us and helping us survive but as adults, it is now our responsibility to make friends with our ego and our sub-personalities. When we make peace with the disowned parts of ourselves, we begin to reclaim our personal power and take control of our lives.

Most people live like this until they are 35 to 40 years old. A few wake up earlier, but the vast majority do not even know there is another path to take or another way to live. They live out their lives in the illusion that their lives cannot be changed. But they are living an illusion—that this is the only way life can be for them.

You did not enter this life to suffer. You entered it to experience joy, have fun, and make soul enlightenment your path.

Where are you now and in your journey at this point in your life? You have a lot of ground to cover and much to learn. The only problem is that most people want to skip over the early part of their life and enter a new life without building a solid foundation.

Universal Law will not allow you to jump into spiritual enlightenment without going through the proper steps. You have to close the chapter on your childhood, but you cannot do it without clearing the lessons that you came into this life to learn. You signed a contract with the Lords of Karma before entering this life. They gave you all the directions for how to clear the path. Your teacher was charged to make sure you got the lessons.

Everyone has to let the old self from the past die and pass away. We cannot be reborn until we clear the lessons and file them in the archives. Being reborn is not at all as the fundamentalist Christians describe it. It is actually going through a process of re-programming the subconscious mind and letting go of the past with no blame, anger, or fear. It requires us to release all the people who participated in our lives up to this moment, loving and forgiving them for any harm and trauma they have caused you. Give them full permission to love and forgive themselves, also. It may seem that this is not possible in some cases, but it must be done.

Everyone is our teacher, playing right into our lessons. We do the best we can based on the interpretation we make and the information we have, no matter what has happened. We only have one choice; to forgive and love them, then release them to God's divine plan. We will learn the lesson when we are ready to do so. When we do this, we let the old self die and go through rebirth. When we go through the second initiation, we can lock up all the old records, programs and patterns from the past in the archives of our subconscious mind.

It may feel and look like you are making progress, but quite often this is an illusion. You have to get back to the base cause, core beliefs, and core issues. You may not know what they are but they are available by accessing the records. You could have programs that are protecting programs. If that is happening, you have to get through the fear causing the denial. And denying your denial will leave you believing that you are making progress when, in fact, you're really only treading water. *If this is the case, no one is going to be able to tell you or show you anything.* You will claim you have the truth, and that is the way it is.

Many people have traveled through many lifetimes standing still. You start each life where you left the last one. You carry your programs and core beliefs forward to the next life. Beliefs are very strong; they drive your life. The stumbling block is that beliefs will totally misinform you about what is real. You may follow the belief, feeling you have made all the necessary progress only to find yourself falling back when a crisis comes up and catalyzes a lesson.

Life is like a slot machine. You may feel it is a gamble but you can win if you are willing to invest and put quarters in the machine. Fear of vulnerability may be your stumbling block. When you commit yourself to spend the time on the lessons, it pays off. Some people put more quarters in the machine of life so they get more out. But playing the slot machine of life is no gamble. You do the work and you reap the rewards. Teachers are always available to help you, but you have to ask and discipline yourself to follow through. The depth and amount of the lesson you have to work through will determine the difficulty of your journey.

Life is also like a football game. You get a stipulated number of "time-outs." A lesson comes up and you ask for a time-out because you feel you're not ready to handle it. So, you don't have to deal with the lesson now, but it will come up again. When you run out of time-outs, you will have to deal with the lesson. And if you try to take a time-out when there are none left, you will precipitate an illness, disease, or some other dysfunction. *It has to be taken care of now; you do not have any choice.*

If you feel like your life is in chaos, then you have not dealt very well with the lessons, and you are out of time-outs. When you are at the two yard line with no more time-outs, you have to go for the goal. If you choose not to respond to the lesson, it will degenerate into a life-threatening disease. When the lesson gets to this point, there is no turning back. You have to look out for number one, nobody else will. Thinking that someone will take care of you when you're down is delusion.

You are the lead player in your play. To stay in the lead, you have to take control and become the director, too. When you do this, everything will open up. The only challenge before you is to step up and take responsibility for your life. Most people prefer to be led by a teacher, guru, or some person who they think will show them the way. True teachers do not want followers; they will show you, or light the way. Then they will release you and expect you to create your own path. No one can clear your lesson or take it away for you. If they tell you they can, they are creating karma for themselves.

Many books offer you insight as to your path but you have to blaze the trail. As the number of trailblazers increases, the faster the consciousness will expand. We are starting to approach the effect of the Hundredth Monkey Theory as put forward by Ken Keyes. He reported that monkeys on a small island discovered that potatoes tasted better if they washed them before eating them. More monkeys began to wash their potatoes, and suddenly the practice reached a critical mass such that monkeys on the next island began doing the same thing. The theory is that if enough monkeys practice a particular behavior, critical mass is reached and the behavior spreads exponentially. This now has been proven with a number of research projects.

This is beginning to happen in the field of spiritual growth and enlightenment. Have you been touched by the Hundredth Monkey Theory? Many people believe that this means we will have a mass ascension and release of karma. This is not my information, however. We have to wash our potatoes on our own first. We have to do the work. We cannot jump over our childhood and forget the lessons we came to learn. We chose our parents in order to learn from them, or teach a lesson to them.

Workshops, seminars, lectures, books, and tapes present many processes that claim to change your life. Do they work? The only way to know is to candidly evaluate your life before, during, and after you participate in the process. Did real measurable change occur?

The only proof of any process is in its effect on your life in the years following. Many of us will hang onto a program even after we know it's not working but a "known is often better than going into the unknown." Just remember the following:

Fear is "False Evidence Appearing Real." Fear is feeling as if you have no power or control over a situation. Anger is an attempt to regain power and/or control.

Ask yourself these questions:
- Am I happier than last year?
- Do I have more joy in my life now?
- Do I have harmonious relationships with most people?
- Do I have true peace in my life?
- Do I have unconditional love and acceptance now?
- Do I have an abundance of financial prosperity?
- Can I approach everyone in my life without fear or anger?
- Do I try to avoid people or situations that I feel will upset me?
- Do I need to have authority in a situation?
- Do I try to control conversations, activities?
- Do I feel that I have to be better than or one up on other people?
- Am I afraid that others will "do" something to me?
- Do I feel I can say what I feel to others?
- Can and will I speak the truth?
- Am I critical of myself and of others, their behavior, beliefs, or attitudes?
- Would I rather follow a standard, or make my own decision?
- Do I need friends and support around me, or can I be alone?

The New Millennium will require you to be an individual rather than a follower. In evaluating your soul growth, you may need help. If you are laboring under a false belief, it can cause all kinds of problems. You can assume that you've mastered many of the lessons and initiations but since your assumptions are based on beliefs or interpretations which may not be not accurate, knowing calls for some kind of reality check

Your conscious mind drives your life with inaccurate beliefs and a belief held for a period of time becomes a built in program telling you "the way things are." How committed are you are to holding onto the way you *think things are* rather than opening to the way *things really are*? The body/mind will always tell the truth.

The subconscious mind is a computer that doesn't need any particular viewpoint on a subject but just feeds back whatever is on file. By checking for the reality of a situation, you can get both the belief and the reality on the subject. The best way is to have a person who has no need to prove a point with you check you with kineseology, or muscle testing. You can also use this method to discover if you have lessons to deal with particular issues in your life. The major question that we need to test for first is whether the body is switched and electromagnetic polarity balanced. To get an accurate answer you have to be in your body with the electromagnetic field moving in the proper direction. All these test procedures are described in a companion book, *Accessing Your Akashic Records* (available from the Wellness Institute).

The biggest block we have to clarity is honesty with self. Breaking the denial and illusion can be very tricky if your need to be right is locked in. If we *want* to believe a particular point, there is no way anybody will change that belief. The middle-self keeps the illusion of fear of loss of power and control in denial, therefore, it has a vested interest in being right.

If we acknowledge the denial, we have to deal with fear of giving away our power by admitting that we are in the wrong. If we need to stay on top of everything by control, we will be pushed into survival when we try to overcome the need to be an authority. It is extremely threatening to give up control and authority. If people justify their behavior as right for them, they will ignore anyone pointing out to them their faulty reasoning.

When I refer to middle-self, I am not indicating any connection with ego. For 20 years, I assumed that ego was actually middle-self.

However, I have finally come to understand who manipulates the mind. I have now discovered that middle-self has three basic subdivisions: Conscious Rational Decision Making Mind (CRDMM), Instinctual Mind (IM), and Conscious Irrational Mind (CIM).

The sub-personalities are in the CIM, an area of the mind without the ability to make rational decisions. It operates from the sub-personalities and the beliefs that are programmed into it. The qualities that we have described as ego in the past are actually sub-personalities that control our lives. Beliefs and interpretations are stored in middle-self, automatic pilot operates from middle-self programs, and all self-talk comes out of middle-self. Middle-self can access subconscious mind, but subconscious mind does not make any decisions. It is basically a data storage bank for which ego is the librarian. It is not the villain that we have made it out to be.

As I work with sub-personalities that drive the middle-self, I often find a denial sub-personality driving the core belief or the base program. It usually operates from fear and seems stronger than the basic sub-personality. Sometimes they will back up on each other, causing denial of denial. In this case, it is useless to even begin to try to make a point or discuss a situation because clients cannot even understand the concept to begin with since their minds will deny that the situation even exists. With this denial driving clients totally into illusion, it sets up a "denial of denial" sub-personality. When I try to point out the client's abnormal or dysfunctional behavior, the denial of denial causes him or her to justify and project back on me.

Clarity and honesty with integrity is one of the hardest lessons to overcome because we operate out of fear and insecurity. The journey to enlightenment can have many boulders on the trail to stop us, but we can get around them if we are willing to clear the blocks to our transformation.

Most people respond to such a confrontation by feeling threatened, and when we feel threatened, we will go into fight, flight, or shut down. In fight, we will defend, justify and deny; in flight, we run away from the illusory cause of our fear; in shut down, we pull in and hide from everything.

A reality check will reveal the truth of the matter. But even then, the middle-self may block truth so that the sub-personalities can play games. The disowned selves will block clarity and steer you away from the truth. You'll think that you're making accurate decisions, but misreading reality will give you the inappropriate direction. When we get our team to work together with the same goals, we can make major progress. But aligning the team to a common purpose takes commitment to release the vows of limitation that we have taken in the past.

There are also issues with implants, cords, and attachments. They can be controlled by discarnate entities, aliens, and inter-dimensional beings. Spirit possession is a major issue with most people now. Each emotional trauma creates an opening for them to attach. There are 25 potential sub-personalities, each one with a gate-keeper to keep the lesson open. Major behavior programs connected with sub-personalities open gates, or doors[1]. Such programs include I'm not okay, judgment, jealousy, control, authority, and manipulation. Gate-keepers will be assigned to these doors until you get the lesson. The gate-keeper can be taken over and replaced by a demonic or possessive being who will control and move in. They may speak for you without you knowing it; it happened to me many times. If we rush to judgment and cannot understand why, these beings will keep you in turmoil with anger, fear, and karmic saboteurs to get you in a disassociated state.

I've never worked with people who have been clear from the beginning. Many times karmic guards will replace karmic gate-keepers to protect or enforce vows, oaths, and allegiances that we've taken in past lives, or curses and hexes that were placed on us in past lives. They have to be removed and sent to the spiritual plane.

In the 1980s, we found very few problems with possession. As we move closer to the New Millennium shift, I see more attacks by inter-dimensional beings trying to stop the shift, or destroy our ability to make the shift. At this point, we are winning the battle, moving toward the New Millennium at an ever-accelerating rate. At some point, we will make a quantum leap through the barrier and there will be no more resistance. When we break through to the Fifth Dimension, we will be above the Astral Plane, so astral beings will not be able to enter our sphere. As of now, the date of the breakthrough will be after the year 2000 but it could come earlier if our transformation speeds up.

It is important that we work together in this shift. To make it, we have to be honest with ourselves. The deeper we are in illusion, the more we open ourselves to attachment by possessive entities.

Any kind of drug (even prescription drugs if they affect the mind), including alcohol, will open you up to attachment. We have found that the implants can cause neurological dysfunctions. When removed, the symptom goes away.

Pleiadian implants can have active programs attached, such as those that jam the electrical functions of the neurological system causing it to malfunction. Some operate like transponders in airplanes that transmit location so your movements can be tracked. However, few Andromedans use implants. Their tools are mind control and manipulation of programs.

I continually evaluate my position and how I respond to people. For example, I find that my "judger sub-personality" is self-righteous and very active but I have a handle on it now. It feels great to get in control of that aspect of me. Since I am aware of how I respond, I can detect and control it.

When you first encounter spiritual evolution and transformation, evaluating your journey is very important. You can do this by keeping a journal until you can evaluate each situation as it comes up. When you can let go of the need to react in a certain way, you're on the path. When you gain control of all your responses and can respond without fear, anger, jealousy, manipulation, self-righteousness, and the need to control or be in the right, you are on your path to enlightenment. (My book for apprentice Earth Masters, *Being a Spiritual Being in a Physical Body*, delineates this process.)

[1]This concept comes from Transactional Analysis.

5

The Battle for Clarity

THE NEW MILLENNIUM REQUIRES US to take stock of where we are on our life path. You did not come to this Earth Plane to get into competition or suffer. You were not forced to incarnate. There are no victims; it is all free choice. Everyone at some time asks, "Why am I here?" You are not here to work, have children, or deal with the routine of everyday life. You are here for one reason only: soul growth and evolution. The physical realm is the *only* place you can learn the lessons and make that growth.

When you are between lives, you can see clearly the path and the lessons on the path. When you get in a body, however, the journey can become blurred, and the directions lost. You have a teacher, however, that will help recover the map and directions to the lessons if you are willing to listen and take down the information. Who is this teacher? Not in a body on the physical plane. It took me 41 years to catch on, recognize the message, and get in contact with my teacher. When I got it, I went full steam to find the way. It took me another 17 years to clear the way.

With this basic experience, I am able to show you the short cuts, so you can do it in a fraction of the time it took me. And you are in control of the "correspondence course" with your Higher Self and your teacher. I am not saying that I have the whole pie, but I have yet to meet anyone who has more pieces. If I do, I will add them to my pie.

The question your teachers will ask you is, "Do you get it?" They are reevaluating the basic agreement you made with them before you were born in this body. They are very aware of your soul evolution. Your teachers are not asking you for *their* information, they know exactly where you are. What they want you to know is whether or not *you* can recognize where you are in your journey to enlightenment, or if you have the truth versus illusion and denial.

In the final evaluation, your teacher will make the decision as to where you are and will inform you as to what you have to do to get it. And this "it" is what my books are about. You will be given plenty of support and help when you get it. You have all the resources at hand when you understand how to access them. *But you have to do the work.*

To enter the New Millennium and to make soul progress, we must clear all the lessons in the third-dimensional reality. All the emotional trauma must be cleared, along with all the fear that "I'm not okay" and the lack of self-worth programming. You have to reclaim your personal power. Self-esteem and internal validation are the most important qualities. You can be in denial and illusion while your mind's beliefs will convince you that you have handled your issues. However, you can't jump over the lessons of physical existence.

Many people try to avoid dealing with the emotional and mental plane lessons and jump into spiritual plane lessons without clearing the body/mind of fear-based lessons. To do so puts major stress on the body and will continually pull you back to physical plane lessons. As the disciple Matthew stated, "Ye must be as little children before you can enter the kingdom of God." To do so, you have to attain complete clarity. Children are not born with fear. We take their power from them and teach fear to them, fear of loss of control and power.

During the writing of this book, we were looking for any programs, situations or patterns that would hold us back and sabotage our transformation. We discovered that each emotional trigger has programs connected to it in ways we had not found before. In the 12 doors you go through in the enlightenment process, you also have 12 lessons that continually repeat at each door. This we knew was accurate. We discovered that there are 25 gates connected with each emotional trigger[1]. Each has a gate-keeper connected with it to keep it open until you let go of the emotion, such as judgment, envy, control, or self-righteousness.

When we tried to close the gate after we released the program, we found that many of the gate keepers had been replaced with Astral Plane beings from the Dark Forces. Some were demonic. As we dug deeper, we found that they were protecting and enforcing curses or hexes placed in a past life. On checking further, we found vows, oaths, and allegiances from past lives that were connected with the curses. Not only were they trying to keep the door open, they were also invoking the curses and trying to control a person's behavior with the emotional triggers and the vows, oaths, and allegiances. In the process, they can activate sub-personalities.

We found up to seven levels deep, depending on the length of connection with the Dark Forces, alien forces, or the Luciferian forces. This proved to be a major breakthrough in clearing negative aspects from a person. We have not seen one person who has not had some connection with the Dark Forces. It seems that all of us have a negative side that has to be cleared, along with all the curses, hexes, vows, oaths, and allegiances that we took when we were participating with them. (See Appendix B for more information and a process to clear possession.)

In my life, these breakthroughs have proven invaluable. They have turned my life around 180 degrees. I am finding that the Astral Plane forces have tried to literally kill me because I am their number one enemy. The curses and hexes that were placed on me were the major obstacles blocking my path. Apparently, I had been a very high ranking officer in the Dark Forces for many thousands of years. My renouncing them and turning to the Light was a major problem for them, because I knew all their tricks and methods. The fact that I had developed a process to clear people of the control of the Dark Forces really infuriated them. The processes we use to clear a person of implants and possession by the Dark Forces work 100 percent, and they know it.

Due to the fact that I was the target, I needed something to protect me, so we invented and developed the Body/Mind Harmonizer. Using Tesla information about coils and scalar waves, we created a small box about the size of a garage door opener which will protect the wearer from all Dark Force beings who try to place implants, or get into you and affect you. Not only does the device protect you, it sets up an earth frequency harmonic field 15 feet in diameter. This will cause your body to identify with 12 hertz, providing a screen for stress. Many people function at higher frequency (40 to 90 hertz) which is very damaging to the body and will eventually push it into adrenal exhaustion. As you get comfortable with the box frequency, your body will begin operating at the 12 hertz. You will notice the stress you are subject to and begin functioning at that frequency.

People have described the Body/Mind Harmonizer as electronic medicine and many claim they no longer need mind-altering drugs. (Appendix C gives more information about the unit.)

You may have to do a reality check to see where your interpretations are overrunning the truth. Breaking through the illusions is very hard if denial is locked in. Do you live in peace, happiness, harmony, and joy with unconditional love and financial abundance? Are you able to deal with all situations that arise without fear or anger? Are your Inner Critic, Judger, and Pleaser sub-personalities under control? Do you run away from situations or people you feel you cannot control or cannot deal with? Can you speak your feelings and tell the truth without fear of rejection? Can you accept all people without judgment?

My path had a lot of boulders and canyons in it for over twenty years. Even up to January, 1996, I couldn't understand why I was having so much trouble in my life since I had committed myself to working for the higher beings. When I was ignorant of Spiritual Principles and Universal Laws, I had fewer problems in my life. I got angry many times and tried to quit. "If I cannot stop this negative flow of garbage in my life, I am not going to continue."

When I cooled down each time, my teacher would lecture me about how I had to find the lessons myself. I would get help if I would do as I was told. Being a controlling counter-dependent, I felt I had to do it all myself. I was not willing to let other people tell me what to do. When I finally overcame that program, I started getting help. How often do we run from the very people who can help us?

As long as people did not violate my programming, I was willing to work with them. When I got the truth, I finally started getting help—from the very people to whom I'd taught Neuro/Cellular Repatterning (see Chapter 11). When we cleared the encoded and encrypted programs, my life turned around. I feel I finally have crested the mountain. Everything that I do seems to be falling into place now that I have recovered the full message: "I'm all right no matter what others may think or feel. I have no need to justify who I am. I am entitled to peace, happiness, harmony, joy with acceptance, unconditional love, and an abundance of financial prosperity."

I am in full control, now that I've reclaimed my personal power on all levels of my existence. Now that I have taken full responsibility for myself, nobody can deny me this opportunity. We can fool ourselves very easily with this one. The inner self and holographic mind know the true answer. All we have to do is use Behavioral Kinesiology to test ourselves.

[1]We discovered this information while researching NC/R experiences. The twelve doors of the enlightenment process are described in my book, *Journey into the Light*.

The Battle
for Your Mind

IN 1984, I WROTE AN article for our newspaper, *The Catalyst*, subtitled, "Privacy, Individual Freedom, Creativity and the Future." In 1984, we were patting ourselves on the back, saying, "See, we handled it, George Orwell was wrong." I am not so sure about that now. In hindsight, it seems that Orwell was more right than wrong in his predictions when he wrote *1984*. In 1940, Orwell lived in a totalitarian world dominated by Hitler, Mussolini, and Franco and he saw a different world. But when we evaluate his views, based on what has happened up to the present, the similarities are frightening. His projections of his 1940s world into the future assumed that fascism would establish a stronghold in the world, and it scared him enough to write a book about his theory.

Aldous Huxley explored the same subject in *Brave New World*. At the time, his book was considered science fiction, but the portrait of the future he painted seems more upsetting when we look at the potential of it coming true. With companies now experimenting with plant and human genetics and animal cloning, his concepts are no longer science fiction.

Today, scientists are working with nanotechnology, a new frontier where they can take the cellular structure apart, atom by atom, insert new programming at the cellular level, then reassemble the cellular structure with the new programming. They even claim that they can put a blood scavenger in a person's bloodstream that will destroy disease from the cellular level.

Today, there is talk about putting a microchip under a newborn's skin so as to identify him or her in the event of kidnapping. It could also store electronically his or her entire medical history for doctors in the event of an emergency situation that rendered the child unconscious. This is already normal for Air Force pilots on the grounds that it protects the heavy financial investment made in training a pilot. If they go down, they can be found because orbiting satellites can detect the homing device signal. When a US pilot went down in Bosnia in 1995, the official reason for his rescue was that he cleverly put out signs so that U.S. searchers could locate him but enemy troops could not. However, according to a radio interview with a military search and rescue team member, locating him in that area would have been impossible without something guiding them.

Take a good look at our society and the way we willingly give away our power, allowing government to expand and take more control each year. Many people want Big Brother to take responsibility for almost everything. They are willing to sell out their freedom for more benefits. Power tends to corrupt in any organization. The more manipulation that goes on in governments and corporations, the more control they get. And due to apathy and neglect on our part, we know very little about what goes on behind the scenes.

We may be falling headlong into Big Brother's grip, as most of us do not understand or recognize the effects inherent in governmental control. The apathy of people toward government and politics is astounding. The politics of corporate and government control and manipulation of the media is amazing. We can't get a clear picture of what is going on in the world. Corporate disdain for the environment and people's welfare is alarming. There is very little difference between Big Brother today and the past. However, today, Big Brother has very sophisticated electronic surveillance and computers that can track the entire population effortlessly.

Big Brother makes a few mistakes from time to time, as revealed in the Kennedy assassination, the Nixon impeachment, and now the Clinton fiasco. But as each setback disappears, forgotten by history with no one rising in protest, they get a little bolder.

The government is, however, getting worried by the militia movement. The Ruby Ridge/Randy Weaver and Waco/Branch Davidian conflicts were tests to see if they could strong-arm people and get away with it. There seems to be no remorse or moral redress over the fact that many people were killed and that people's rights were unjustifiably and illegally abridged. A small minority of people are beginning to get the message; talk shows are starting to wake people up. In fact, Congress tried to pass legislation to ban talk shows from discussing politics.

The Oklahoma City bombing and the Arizona Amtrak derailment are two more examples of the government engineering a major threat to generate fear as support for drafting legislation that would dramatically curb the freedom of individuals. Few people know of the flurry of unpublicised, far-reaching Executive Orders that came out of the Oklahoma City bombing. Those in power will stop at nothing to get what they want. The Dark Forces have infiltrated the government and no ethical or moral considerations will stop their push for total control.

The real culprit is never revealed because Big Brother puts up a fall guy to take the rap for the mistake. The Shadow Power behind those in power is set on one track: covert takeover. Those who do not follow the rules pay the price with their lives. Once someone knows the inside story, he cannot back out. Vince Foster paid the price. That case is not closed, and with more revealed, we find that he was just on the surface. Timothy McVeigh and Terry Nichols are the two most recent fall guys, one sentenced to life, the other death. This has been going on in Government for 80 years. It turned around in 1994 but the message is still the same: "Take responsibility." Yet, the lofty ideals of freshmen congressmen never materialize.

Why do so many congressional people drop out or resign? There is a movement beneath the surface government that reveals to many of the top political figures what damaging information is known about them and warns them that if they don't leave quietly, it will be made public. Using the government's own intimidation tactics on them works well—the covert actions of this small, well-organized group is beginning to pay off.

The 1992 election was a wake up call in which many of the elected representatives got the wrong message. Republicans were voted out because of who they were. People were fed up and rejected the incumbents but the message has yet to penetrate the government.

Heads are beginning to roll as the information gets to the people. One of the most blatant abuses of power was the appointment of Larry Potts to be second-in-command at the FBI. He was the agent in charge during the Ruby Ridge fiasco. He has since been demoted and suspended after the congressional hearings. More heads will roll as the people begin to take responsibility and step up to take control.

Computer technology, instant global communication via satellites and the Internet, huge computer data bases, social security numbers, credit cards, bank account numbers, and credit reporting agencies means that all information about you is instantly accessible anywhere in the world. The 1995 move for national health care was a cover to get a national ID card on everybody. The IRS wanted to be able to track a person's lifestyle so they could determine if they were paying the appropriate taxes.

What would have happened if the Nazi war machine had had these tools and technology? Even without computers and data bases, they still succeeded in genocide. Hitler was an accomplished metaphysician and used all the tools available to gain control. He manipulated the minds of an entire nation to get people to give up their power and the majority of the population accepted it. Are we going to fall into the same mold?

It seems that people are starting to wake up now, but the majority of the population falls into five categories:

1. The *Greedy* who want power and money
2. The *Victims* who see no way out of their dilemma
3. The macho *Sports Fans* who live their lives outside themselves by allegorically projecting through sports figures
4. The *Majority*, the large silent group who do not have any identification and live their lives with no direction
5. The *Aware*, currently a tiny minority but rapidly expanding in number.

Orwell raised an important issue that goes to the core of current Western thought. Can individual freedom and privacy survive the onslaught of modern western technology? Huxley was less optimistic in his outlook, because he felt that Big Brother would take over everything in time. We would sell out our power to "soulless automatons." Many people would do that now if they could get cradle-to-grave security and not have to think or take responsibility. We are in the Information Age, and if we refuse to acknowledge it, subliminal programming will take over and cause us to give away our personal power through fear. If we live on automatic pilot and let ego take over, we will live in survival, and it will permeate every facet of our lives.

The school boards and state education departments are making a successful attempt to install Goals 2000 in the schools in many states. The research was funded by corporate think-tanks and major corporations. Pioneered by psychologist Carl Rogers and his colleagues, the concept was to get children to interact on a feeling level, to discuss personal activities and multi-cultural programs. It plays down learning the basics of education such as math and reading. However, it has degenerated into a program to teach children to take orders and follow routines rather than think creatively. As a result, teaching the three R's has been supplanted by how to interact in society according the psychologists' formula. Teachers are told to teach down to the lowest common denominators in the classroom, so in classes with multi-racial integration and language barriers, very little is accomplished in the way of learning.

The result is that intelligent children are bored and become trouble-makers in the classroom. They are being grouped with the real troubled children who are learning disabled. Unless children are very motivated, this treatment affects their self-esteem and self-worth. I have seen children in my practice with these emotional problems. They have to be sent to private schools to avoid the problem of public schools.

The creators of Goals 2000 are now speaking out publicly in seminars and on radio stations. Unfortunately, the program is out of their hands. The liberal teacher establishment likes the program because it gives them more control over the teaching methods and control over resisters. They are installing it in schools as fast as they can, so we can expect the education of our children in public schools to decline.

Already, we see reading and writing skills in decline. Children are being set up for mind control. As a result we are experiencing a direction-less generation of children already and Goals 2000 is not yet even fully in place. Fortunately, children with thinking minds will resist manipulation, and we will see light shining through those that do.

1984 came and went, yet we seem to have our freedom. Orwell's point was that pervasive, insidious, oppressive political regimes control our lives. The difference now is that with computer technology, you appear in many data banks with complete files on who you are, and how you live your life, and how you spend your money. Of course, the less you use their data-gathering tools such as credit cards and bank accounts, the more freedom you will have. Pacific Bell boasts the advent of new information technology that will yield even more access to "private information." In fact, there is no longer such a thing as privacy. Orwell never dreamed of such advances in his time; what would he say now?

All is not lost. We do have a vocal minority watchdog that calls the government to task, and with the advent of talk radio, it is expanding at a quantum rate. They want to take responsibility and return honesty, ethics, and integrity in communication to business and government. These people value their personal freedom, safety, and privacy. They refuse to be controlled by fear and are willing to stand up for what they believe in. In the past few years, Big Brother has tried to move in and test to see if we will take up the cause; we have shown them we will but they don't yet have the full message; they're only becoming aware of the movement now.

Are you willing to make a commitment to take personal responsibility and discipline yourself to follow through consistently with new consciousness? That is what the New Millennium requires. That is what it will take to transition to the New Millennium. Are you willing to stand up for what you believe in and take total control of your life? What this world needs is peace, love, and caring—not fear, anger, greed, and manipulation. We are making more headway each year.

In retrospect, I feel more confident now than I did in 1984 when I wrote the original article. Communism has less influence and totalitarian governments are losing their control. People are questioning government action at all levels. Radio shows such as Art Bell's *Coast To Coast* have really awakened the politicians to the fact that there are people out there that are not controllable by the media, and they are telling the truth about how the government has tried to control our sources of information.

The ultimate tool for control was demonstrated 30 years ago in movie theaters when a subliminal message would appear on the screen just before the intermission, saying, "Buy and eat popcorn." The sales of popcorn went up over 50% each time the message appeared. Any visual media can control you without your conscious awareness. Our eyes are a direct channel to our mind and the powers in government and business know that. Subliminal sounds will do the same thing.

At a Broadway play in New York 25 years ago, the unexpected happened. During the play, one of the actors played a didgerridoo, an Australian horn. The problem was that the horn was made here and not in Australia. It was not tuned to the proper octave range. It was tuned to the exact frequency that governs the sphincter muscle. Everyone in the audience and backstage defecated on the spot.

Our computers, too, are subject to many control factors of which we are unaware. The lesson is to detach as much as possible and take control of your life so other people and agencies cannot influence your mind. However, the mass of the population would willingly trade their rights and freedom for benefits.

Instead of being concerned with these people, we must concern ourselves with the spiritual individuals seeking enlightenment. Unfortunately, many of them, too, will give up their personal power for the promise of help in achieving enlightenment. Knowing the rules does not get you there. Reclaiming your personal power and taking responsibility does.

Eric Hoffer's book, *True Believer*, is a classic on mass movements and how people become joiners and followers of religions, cults, gurus, human potential speakers, and supposedly enlightened teachers. His feeling was, "True believers are not intent on bolstering and advancing a cherished self. They are craving to be rid of the unwanted self. They are followers, not because of a desire for self-control and self advancement, but because it satisfies their passion for self-renunciation." Hoffer also added that, "true believers are eternally incomplete and insecure." The disowned self that is so uncomfortable to deal with will be repressed to the point that the person doesn't even know it is part of him because he or she is operating in a state of illusion. Quite often, people become so caught up in a group or movement that they become brainwashed without knowing it. Many leaders, teachers, and preachers will describe it as a "conversion" in which they are being "saved" from themselves and the devil or whoever.

The old church used accusations and guilt to control people. "You're a sinner, you're destined for hell if you do not do this, that, or whatever." This is not a new phenomenon. All that is needed is an authority figure who can use the basic forms of control: the voice roll technique, music with a repetitive beat at 45 to 72 beats per minute, an eyes-open alpha state and the masses are hypnotically lulled into security. Fundamentalist revival preachers use it very effectively as do many cults and spiritually oriented groups. And Hitler was a master; watch old newsreel of the Nuremberg rallies.

The military use a process called "breaking down and rebuilding." The same technique was used by Werner Erhart and his trainers in EST seminars. Cults do the same thing to get control of a person. When something is offered that will give a person some form of awareness, even if it is an illusion, people will be drawn to it. Most of us are sheep who will follow the leader even if we do not know where he is going. People who are unwilling to subject themselves to this type of treatment will be discharged from the military, or banned from such groups.

I meet many seekers who never seem to find the bliss they seek. They will try to convince you that they are seeking "the true self within" or some such. That is the only place the answers are. Some have told me that I am not spiritual because I do not buy their theory, and they go off to seek their true self with someone who will give them the dogma and control their lives. I am not interested in controlling anyone. I want to set them free. The "true believers" do not want to be free. Self-actualization is not their path, even though they tell you it is. They want to give their power away. They look for answers, meaning, acceptance, and validation outside themselves.

Why are those teachers, channels, preachers, and gurus who offer salvation often so successful? People are looking for direction from outside themselves. Rather than looking within and developing their own communication link, they look outside themselves. People will pay anything for salvation. Put a price on it and they will pay it. Take a good look at the conservative, fundamentalist religion movement and the money they have to build large churches and support TV programs. Closer to home, look at the huge success of J.Z. Knight and Ramtha. It was a flash in the pan for a few years, but while it lasted she made millions of dollars. If you have the truth, many people will avoid you because they want a panacea that will give them a feeling of community. Many are so alone that they will do anything, go to any meeting, just to be with someone. Price is not a problem; they will pay it.

The sellers of shamanism, ascension, and spiritual enlightenment are always looking for followers that will accept their concepts without question. In the seminars I have attended, I have found that most of the teachers and leaders truly believe what they are promoting. Quite often, their teaching has merit, but most of the time, people do not get the total picture.

For example, a friend of mine was involved with a group who told her to leave everything in God's hands. She did, but it didn't seem to work. For years, she was committed to the practices but God didn't seem to respond to her needs. Crisis started to manifest in her life. Her chronic fatigue got worse and even the teacher's healing work failed to work. But she was convinced that her life would turn around if only she continued the practices. She was constantly reassured that she was on the path to ascension. The teacher suggested that she try more heath products and become a total vegetarian. She finally slipped into a "wide awake coma" and could barely function. None of the healing that the group did with her had any effect, and she slipped away, finally passing from the physical plane. It was as if she pulled back from life when her path did not work. She was not willing to accept the failure of her program, nor was she willing to change.

The next example happened so fast it boggled my mind. One Saturday, I was talking with a young woman at a weekend retreat entitled the Ascension Celebration at Mt. Shasta, California. She seemed quite normal and was happy to be there. She attended many seminars and had readings by people who had said she was a highly enlightened person and that this was her last lifetime on this planet. I questioned this statement.

The following Wednesday, I was seeing clients at the home of a friend. Sudden I heard him cry out, which was unlike him. He told me that he had just heard that the young woman had been found dead. Apparently, she had planned to meditate using a method that had been taught at the celebration. The following morning, her roommate noticed that she was still sitting up in bed, so she didn't disturb her. When the roommate came home from work that evening, she noticed that the young woman wasn't breathing and was cold to the touch. She called the paramedics who pronounced her dead.

My friend was very disturbed because the young woman had seemed fine at the celebration. He asked if I would communicate with her and find out what happened. I did so and found a very puzzled and upset soul that was trying to get back into the body but couldn't. I explained to her that meditating with the intention to ascend caused her to leave her body through the solar plexus. It is a one-way door that souls take upon death of the body. It is not accessible from outside the body in the fourth dimension, so once you leave the body, you can't get back in. She was out of body and her body was dead.

The so-called "enlightened" teachers had failed to tell her that she had better check out her soul level evolution before she attempted to ascend. Or could it be that they didn't know what they were talking about. Chalk up one soul who walked out of the body when she was not ready. A very heavy lesson. She is now in the cycle of return and has to go through the whole birth process again. If her level of soul evolution had been advanced enough, she could have walked back into a new adult body and continued on. But I doubt that will happen since she made the mistake of walking out of her body. Her upset and fear turned to anger as she realized she had been misled.

Her mistake was listening to a false shaman, a person who didn't understand ascension and gave her directions that caused her death. That person now has a karmic contract to deal with. If you ascend, you take your body with you in a process described in my book, *Journey Into the Light.*

The directionless person is in the majority. Each day is the same routine treadmill. These are the people controllers and cultists want. They are wandering and don't even know it. The "true believers" make up the majority of the population. Those of us who are willing to take responsibility may be in the minority but, because we carve out our own path, we have a lot of clout.

The more I looked into mind control phenomena, the more I realized that the Dark Forces and some aliens were involved. In looking further, I found that governments were also involved. Scientific mind control began in Germany during the 1930s. After World War II, the U.S. brought all the mind control researchers here to continue their work. And today, it continues in many universities and think tanks such as Rand Corp. and Sandia Labs.

My colleagues and I got into mind control when we began to discover all the implants that people had on them. We now have found implants that have specific purposes to destroy people, track, control, and manipulate. The first one we found was a programmed chip that broadcast, "I want to die." Almost every person I have seen in my practice had one. I had three clients who literally died from the control of that implant.

If you feel unwanted, rejected, invalidated, and not all right, the implant affects the mind and the subconscious sets up a life-threatening disease over you have no control. If the base cause is not located, you will simply die. The survivor self and the instinctual self let go and buy into the program. Since we discovered this type of implant in 1994, not a single client has died.

We also found cords attached by the Dracos and the Orions to control people. These were easy to pull out. The more we investigated the more we discovered a seemingly unending line of implants. We found tracker implants that the Orions used with their computers to track people. Then we found modems through which they could actually send messages to you without your knowledcdge. We uncovered frequency jammers that controlled a person's vibrational level. These were set to slow a person down and not allow the body/mind to rise with the Earth frequency. Frequency jammers also affect a person's hearing. I almost lost my hearing completely from this implant.

People are waking up and taking control of their lives at an ever-increasing rate. The battle for your mind can be won by those aware of the techniques that are used. It takes courage to make the commitment, to stand up and be counted. Fear of rejection is very evident when you stand out from the crowd; however, it seems that more people are willing to take that step and stand up for themselves. Of course, pseudo-spiritual types will always want to follow rather than lead, and leaders will always emerge to lead them as long as they exist. The power brokers will always find their followers.

And this seems to extend into the political arena as well. People are aware of the "Good Ol' Boy Network" now and it is on the downturn. Ross Perot's entry into the presidential race in 1992 brought a new phenomenon to politics, and the fast rise of Steve Forbes from a nobody to a front runner showed that many are fed up with *status quo* government. Let's pray that people will see that government is taking more than it is giving.

When people are hungry, they will choose food over freedom, even though they may be blind to the ultimate cost. But as people's awareness rises, the old way falls as we transition to the New Millennium. Piscean Age control and manipulation will not work in the future. But they will die a hard death because of the greed for control and people's desire to be controlled. As the leaders lose power and control, the result will be fear on both sides. Anger is the attempt to regain or recover power and control and people will fight to regain them. But hopefully, they will find that letting go and giving up the need to control is more empowering and fulfilling than fighting for control.

7

Letting Go of Saturnine Influences

AFTER 200 YEARS OF LIVING under Saturn's energy, in 1994, we saw the effects start to let go. We are also in transition from the Piscean Age to the Aquarian Age. As a result, many people are going to cling harder and tighter to their illusory image of themselves. Feelings of being rejected, invalidated, or not accepted will become more evident for those who feel insecure or unstable. For those in denial, the illusion will be so complete that they will not be able to recognize their own behavior.

It will be quite obvious to those with the eyes to see and the ears to hear, for they will have accepted responsibility and taken command of their lives. It will boil down to the difference between attempting to control a situation in fear and knowing that nobody can threaten your stability or security. When you do not need outside validation, then trust, security, self-worth, and self-esteem are not an issue. The skilled observer who has these qualities has no need to try to control the situation. There is no need for external recognition.

Many will be very attached to their self-definition, their status in the material world—degrees, job, house, car—and identifying with the illusion they have created. They will be driven by the need for recognition and validation rather than from their own choosing. Some will buy their acceptance and validation with hard cash, others by being addicted to helping or supporting activities, groups, or people, often taking on tasks to the point of doing a disservice to themselves.

This will crumble in the coming years; who you are will no longer be a valid identification. We will be moving toward a non-status society. It will be *what* you know and *how* you apply it in your life that will count the most. Being your-Self will be more important than being status-oriented. But a person whose identity depends on outside validation will find this threatening. It will be hard to be your-Self if you need outside validation such as being in front of an audience. If they detect the hidden pleas for acceptance and approval, they will refuse to cooperate.

Saturn energy does not let go very easily. People will cling to national origin and other ethnic groups for security—the root of all civil wars, insurrections and random murders. Many will run from change, not realizing that their ego is driving them away from transformation. Running away, afraid of the change, is not so obvious sometimes. People will react in anger and fear because they feel an impending doom but don't know how to deal with it. So, they will lash out in an effort to reclaim their power.

The Aquarian Age is one of ethics, honesty and integrity. It is here; we have no choice and must deal with it. The new Uranian influence will trigger major societal changes in which the only way we can preserve our freedom is by reclaiming our personal power and recognizing that we are "all right." Nobody took our self-esteem or self-worth; we gave it away. Now we have to reclaim our rights by stepping forward and moving into our power. We must take command of our lives. We are entitled to peace, happiness, harmony, joy, unconditional love, and an abundance of prosperity at all levels of our life. We don't need others to give us validation.

As we recognize our basic responsibilities, we wake up to our power. Consciousness is changing very quickly as people wake up to a clear picture of their future possibilities and opportunities. The intensity of pressure began to shift in 1993, really stepped up in 1996, and will culminate on May 5, 2000. The guidance I have received is to stay put because the Earth changes that are predicted are no longer valid. As of February 2, 1994, the structure was changed (see chapter 2). It seems that my prediction of severe weather, disease, and civil wars is more likely to materialize than the predicted violent Earth changes.

As we move closer to the major shift on May 5, 2000, we are sensing a "Quickening" of time and space. One result of this is an increase in crime and suicide in young people who feel that there

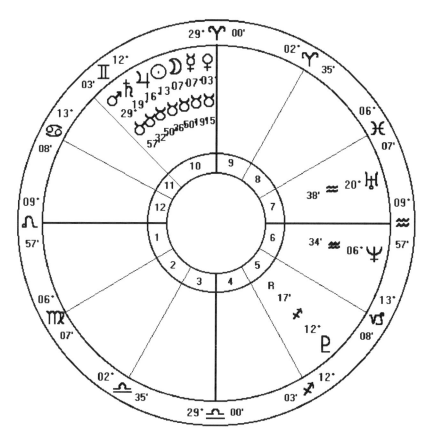

The astrological chart for May 5, 2000 [created using Halloran software]

is no future for them. On the other hand, this is forcing honesty, ethics, and integrity to come to the forefront. Many of the "good ol' boys" in government do not like to see the light shining through their misconduct, but it is destined to happen. The heavy-handed, dishonest police activity is being exposed. The attitude, "I can do anything because I am an authority figure," is crumbling. Many people feel their rights and freedoms are being taken from them. It is a very real truth to those people who feel they are victims.

We create it all. We asked for all we have, even if we cannot remember doing so. We created our life path before we put our first foot on this planet and breathed our first breath. We now have to recognize that unconditional love, compassion, cooperation, and forgiveness are the only way. Life will change when you choose to see the light. Nobody can take your hand and lead you. They can point the way, but you have to take the initiative and make that first step, with the commitment to discipline to stay on the path. We are not blind, and we do not need guide dogs to lead us.

8

The "Jonathan Seagull" Lesson

I T CAN BE AN UNEVENTFUL transition, or a frightful and disturbing experience. We have had the chance to fly for many years, but most people chose security. Risking falling, if you are not able to fly, can be a very scary experience. We've had the opportunity to test our wings since 1988. Most people chose to stay in the nest where it was warm and secure. We do not have a choice now. It is time to "fly or die." If you don't jump to try your wings, you'll never know. This may seem to be an intense statement, but it is the bare truth. We no longer have time to fool around. The call is out. We have to take responsibility for our life path now.

There is not much we can do at the last minute. Since the first wake up call in August, 1987, we have been sliding inexorably down an ever-increasing steep slope and by 2000, we will almost be in freefall. This can be traumatic or smooth; it's your choice. Many people would like to believe that all the work will be done for them. Unfortunately, they will be in for a rude awakening. The slogan of many lightworkers is, "All I need do is follow spirit." Yes, and others may help you, but, as the Bible says, "God helps those who help themselves." We have to open the door. No one is going to do it for us. This is the constant theme throughout my books. It has proven out in my life and the people I have worked with. I am my own laboratory. If the guidance from Source works for me, then I will bring it out in the open.

My feedback is that the slingshot was pulled back in 1994 and released at the beginning of 1995. How was your landing? If you got shot out into an unfamiliar environment, you may have had to scramble for balance. If you were able to fly, you could have glided down to a soft landing. You may have been flying already, so there was very little change in your life. Again, if the illusion is locked in, you may not even notice that time is quickening.

If your belief is that everything is perfectly all right, it will appear that way. There is no need to fly if someone is going to provide you with the vehicle to run away from all the problems. That could be true but for those who choose to stay asleep or put their head in the sand, the cycle of return will continue. We cannot avoid the fact that the only way out is to take responsibility for our future. Many people can state with total commitment to truth in their mind that they totally agree with what I have said, yet turn right around and fall back into their old patterns.

I have found in my practice that over 95 percent of the people who see me as clients have their electromagnetic fields switched or depleted. 90 percent of the people are not functionally in their body/mind's conscious, rational, decision-making mind's control room. There is no way you are going to fly if you are not in the cockpit. Who's going to navigate if you're not there? It may well be a possessive entity, or your ego. If ego has run your life for many years, it may not want to give up control. It has kept you in survival in the past and may feel that that is the only way it can maintain control. We do not want to fight with it to regain control, yet making friends with it may take work.

The only problem is that reality may set in and you may find yourself having to fly without having the lessons first. Learning to fly while you're in a nose dive can be scary. You may find yourself coming in on a wing or a prayer, or worse.

Have a great flight into the New Millennium, Happy landings!

9

The Scientific View

MANY PHYSICISTS TAKE A LARGER world view now that new technology and instrumentation give them a different perspective on the future, and many scientists refuse to subscribe to government cover-ups. Many who held high government positions have gone out on their own with their research, often advancing to the forefront of new discoveries. I have met many of these people at conferences, UFO shows, and various gatherings over the years.

Many of them also contribute to Art Bell's late-night radio show, *Coast To Coast*. This show is heard on over 400 radio stations from 10 p.m. to 3 a.m. (PST), Monday through Friday, and Sunday from 6 to 9 p.m. (PST) and covers a wide range of topics. For example, the pyramids and the ancient ruins left by cultures long departed are perennial subjects of interest. The conservative Egyptologists still cling to the history book accounts of how the pyramids, other buildings, and statuary were built. However, the latest research reveals that the buildings were created by an advanced society with highly advanced technology far beyond what we have today.

A fascinating book by Richard W. Noone, *5/5/2000 Ice: The Ultimate Disaster*, is a virtual compendium of information. In his widespread research about what is predicted for May 5, 2000, Noone contacted a large number of people. One limestone quarry owner said it would be almost impossible to build a structure such as the pyramid of Giza with such large blocks and to fit them together with such exact tolerances (less than two hundredths of an inch) even with today's equipment and knowledge. Further, pyramids all over the world are built to the same proportions using the same formulae. They may be different sizes, but the mathematical formulae are the same.

It seems that not only do clairvoyants, psychics, and many intuitive people agree that there will be a pole shift May 5, 2000; Noone's research indicates that the mathematical formulae indicate the same date. Most of the radical researchers have come to the conclusion that the pyramid of Giza is an observatory used for initiations and rituals. The question of who built them is open.

It is unlikely that Egyptians built the pyramids, or that the Greeks as we know them today built the Acropolis, or that anyone who inhabited Central America built the structures there. Researchers have concluded that they were built by a race of people with very advanced technology. My sources say that the descendants of the Sirian extraterrestrials who built the pyramids formed the Masonic Orders, evidenced by Masonic symbols of the kind found on many of the buildings in various locations around the planet. For some reason, they lost some of the keys to the technology. Could it have been mind control, so that the knowledge would be lost over time and not be revealed? Did this superior race know what was going to happen in the thousands of years to come?

My feedback from the Sirian Council is that, when they left, they set up a time suggestion, similar to what we call hypnotic suggestion, in the minds of those who chose to stay behind so that they would forget the final keys to the technology. Through mind control, they made sure that the knowledge would not be used for negative purposes in the far distant future.

There are many different accounts about what happened 6,000 years ago. Quoting the Bible and many other documents to prove their theory, Christian researchers want you to believe that the earth and humanity are only 6,000 years old. Based on the research and calculations of Archbishop Usher, the Christian world assumed that the world began in 4004 BC.

It is now coming to light that a major supernova explosion of a star in another galaxy which researchers have labeled "Vela-X" occurred approximately 6,000 years ago. It was so intensely bright that it lit up this whole area of the universe. This time frame seems to coincide with accounts of intense light in many of the ancient records.

Robert Temple, author of *The Sirius Mystery* and member of the Royal Astronomical Society of England, believes after many years of scientific research that an advanced race of people from a planet in the system of the double star Sirius visited Earth in the year 4500 BC. (The Egyptian calendar was established in the year 4266 BC.) The rising of the star Sirius took place in the exact location that could be viewed from the Great Pyramid's Grand Gallery at an elevation of 23 degrees. On May 5, 2000, Sirius will be at the same location as it was in 4266 BC, except that then, it was in the southern sky, according to Temple. In the year 2000, it will appear in the northern sky, which may indicate a pole shift around that date.

E.A. Wallis Budge, in his translation of the *Egyptian Book of the Dead*, states that the oldest chapter was found in 4266 BC in a foundation deposit of an ancient temple. Ludwig Borchardt believed that the Egyptian calendar was established on this date using the star Sirius as the beginning point because it has an unvarying cycle of 365.25 days and was a point that could be seen from the Giza Pyramid. George Michanowski, in his book, *The Once and Future Star*, provides startling information about the pyramid and the stars.

Professor Charles H. Hapgood has presented evidence in *The Earth's Shifting Crust* that a major shift in Earth's crust may have taken place at this time. He does not mention the sinking of the Atlantean Continent, but this could tie in with the destruction and sinking of Atlantis. The Noah's Ark story must have happened about this time, as there was massive flooding caused by the crustal shifts. In fact, every ancient civilization has a legend concerning a planetary flood.

Another Hapgood book, *Advanced Civilization in the Ice Age*, indicates that there may have been major shifts in the Antarctic areas during this time. One could speculate that the explosion of Vela-X might have produced such a surge that it dislodged the Antarctic ice, initiating major flooding and possibly a shift of the ice caps. These events could have triggered a pole shift, or some other cataclysmic event.

Many researchers are putting together an amazing amount of information in their particular area of expertise. Very few share with each other, so very little of the information reaches the public. It seems many of them are satisfied to amass the research for their own edification.

SeaWiff, a NASA project used to display its findings on a fascinating website on the Internet. Using satellite-based infrared cameras, they pick up planetary "hot spots" that point to geological stress. Apparently, plate stress has been increasing significantly all over the planet. The so-called "Ring of Fire" around the Pacific Rim appears to be heating up. Magma is rising in many inactive volcanoes and even in places where there are no volcanoes.

One such location creating interest lies in northern Florida, an area not known for activity in the past. Japan is lighting up like a torch and, if it continues, could be ripe for major disaster. Historically, earthquakes and volcanic eruptions have caused many earth shifts. Mt. St. Helens was the first to go off in the present round but many others are rumbling. Mt. Penatubo in the Philippines buried Clark Air Force Base under many feet of ash. The cost of rebuilding it ensured its closure.

In 1883, Mt. Krakatoa in Indonesia exploded with such force that it was heard around the world. In fact, the sound waves went around the world three times. The eruption equaled the force of a 150 megaton bomb and destroyed all buildings and villages within a 100-mile radius. Three tidal waves were formed, one of which reached a height of 131 feet and broke anchor chains on ships moored in the port at Valparaiso, Chile, on the other side of the South Pacific Ocean.

According to Lowell Ponte, a consultant on environmental changes, Krakatoa's tower of ash and smoke rose 50 miles into the sky. Since this was above the cloud level, the ash took more than 25 years to settle out. Some of the ash may still be in the upper atmosphere 100 years later. The eruption was 20 times larger than Mt. St. Helens. It blackened the atmosphere, and totally blocked out the sun 100 miles away. The smoke and particulate matter spread around the planet, reducing the temperature one full degree for two years. Floating pumice was so thick on the ocean's surface for over a 100 miles that you could walk on it and not sink. It dropped ash and rock thirteen feet deep up to 100 miles away. Krakatoa blew out eleven cubic miles of material and three cubic miles of gas, releasing power equivalent to two hundred trillion kilowatt hours, or enough electricity to power the planet for a year. The western U.S. could suffer as much or more from volcanoes and earthquakes if all the nine volcanoes on the West Coast (California, Oregon and Washington) erupted. Those who watch this magma heating say that it will cause some serious earthquakes in the future, probably accompanied by enormous tidal waves. But we have seen how consciousness, if amassed as a force, will change events.

The comet Hale-Bopp changed its course four times in 1995 as it approached Earth. There was a concern that a second comet was discovered in 1995 might crash into this planet. The point of impact was projected to be in the Pacific Ocean. If this had happened, a tidal wave of 400 feet or more in height would cause tremendous floods. But it, too, has apparently changed course and will pass by the planet.

The Effect of the Photon Belt

The earth's magnetic field has been dropping for the last 500 years and will come to a zero point in the year 2000. The effect of dropping to zero point will not be a disastrous vibration when the readjustment of the poles takes place. The theory is that, as we go through the Photon Belt, the field will be readjusted. (The Photon Belt is a mass of highly charged particles of light, but they have no electrical charge.) As Earth approaches the outer edge, the density will increase, causing a very bright light refraction from the particles. As Earth begins to pass through the center of the belt, the density of the particles will be so heavy that it will appear as if are experiencing a solar eclipse.

The Photon Belt has a demagnetizing effect so that no electric, electronic, and magnetic devices will work, allowing the planet to readjust the magnetic field. There is no scientific evidence as to what this belt will do since it has not been experienced in recorded history. So at this point, it is all speculation based on many people's visions and communications with sources outside themselves.

Researchers project that the Earth will take 18 years to go through the Photon Belt. At the time of its discovery in 1961, Earth had already entered the belt's outer reaches. Actual entry started in 1995 and will end in 2013. The period of greatest impact is unknown but it is forecast that we will be in the densest part of the belt for about two weeks and that the most intense influence will last for about one month.

Some people have predicted that we will have blackouts for five days, freezing sub-zero weather, intense light that could blind a person, winds up to 400 miles an hour, plus erratic weather patterns and lighting effects. Before and after that time, life on Earth will be different but not so as to cause major problems. As the north and south poles readjust and shift, the electromagnetic field will stabilize.

The Photon Belt apparently will not trigger the same phenomena this time as it has in the past. However, it could have the psychological effect of pushing people to the edge. It will align our personal electromagnetic fields and force us into a clearing process, much like a spiritual detoxification. Bearing in mind the saying, "The truth will set you free," those who are ready could find it a great gift, whereas those in fear, survival and resistance could experience great trauma.

A major question for researchers studying the polar ice caps is whether the pole shift will upset the ice caps or cause them to slide off the land mass. If they do, they will raise sea level. In *Life and Death of the Planet Earth*, Tom Valentine explains the pole shift as a shift and changing position of the earth's rotational axis in relation to other heavenly bodies. This will cause a sudden relocation of the earth on its axis, without changing position relative to the tilt from the solar orbit. He tells us that the earth is like a round ball spinning in space and, as it spins, it also is wobbling.

The southern polar mass is heavier than the north, which creates an imbalance. This increases the wobble effect as the weight builds up year after year. Eventually, the tilt of the earth can no longer overcome the centrifugal force of the spinning earth. At this critical point, the polar ice masses could be thrown with devastating speed toward the equator. Most civilizations will be destroyed if not by the shock waves then by flooding, as the oceans would rise by up to 600 feet. Valentine and many other scientists are speculating that the last ice age was caused in the same manner.

The earth's resonant frequency has been 7.83 hertz for hundreds of years. In 1993, it began to climb. By 1996, it was up to 9.3 hertz and then 11.6 hertz as of July, 1998, and is increasing by one hertz per year. In fact, the increase seems to be accelerating each year and is projected to top out at 14 hertz. The scientific community cannot understand why the constants they have used in their work for many years are shifting.

Stan Deyo, a frequent guest on the Art Bell Show said that you really don't want to know what the future holds and that it is better that you go on with your life and have a good time. When Art Bell coaxed him into revealing some of the information he was aware of, he discussed his involvement with building circular wing aircraft, also known as flying saucers. It seems that world governments have been involved with saucer-type aircraft since 1952 when officials from the Eisenhower administration met with extraterrestrial groups from the Intergalactic Council to define a project to give the U.S. the technology to build circular-wing aircraft. As a result, we have aircraft that can fly up to 20,000 miles per hour with no noise. They move by sucking themselves along with electromagnetic anti-gravity devices. Apparently, the New World Order has been supporting this research for many years.

Deyo is not the first person to mention that only 50 to 60 percent of our federal defense budget goes to defense, with the balance going to finance undercover "black" projects. Many of the projects involve taking over control of the population. The New World Order proponents are totally under cover, and their intent is to take over and engineer an economy in which no one can travel without the government knowing exactly where they are, how much money they spend, and what they spend it on.

Another example of a black project has come to light through testimony of former employees who have resigned their positions at Los Alamos National Laboratories. They report that aliens in physical bodies are working at the laboratory. According to my sources, they have been there since the 1950s.

I met Phil Schriber at a conference in Seattle in 1995. Over dinner, he talked about his experiences as a physicist at Los Alamos Laboratories for 17 years. He confirmed that aliens worked at the lab. He quit and left the lab under very strange circumstances after he engaged in a verbal battle with an alien who almost killed him. He planned to go public with all the information that had been covered up for years, and undercover agents tried to kill him six times. As proof, he showed me the bullet wounds.

Next, a Japanese corporation asked him to consult with them on some very complex situations. He agreed, but the US Government denied him a visa to travel to Japan. So the corporation sent a chartered jet over to pick him in Canada. When he returned, he was killed in February, 1996 near his home in Oregon. There was no coverage of his death in any newspapers. I found out about his demise at a conference that I was presenting at in October, 1997. My friend Al Beilek told me that the agents finally succeeded. Since I do not want to be a target too, I will not reveal what Phil told me. Those in our Government seem to stop at nothing to prevent their dishonesty being revealed, and Phil is not the only one who has been silenced by death in the last ten years.

Apparently, many scientific researchers know that the governments of our planet are working together with the cover-up of black projects. However, the cover-ups are starting to break down on many fronts. Richard Hoagland has speculated that the government has evidence of off-world cultures that were far more advanced scientifically than ours and that the space shuttle missions have been looking for further evidence of their existence. He also feels that we are now approaching the same point these societies were at when they were destroyed or disappeared.

Dr. Nick Begich, an Alaskan physicist researching the HAARP[1] Project, feels that using HAARP is causing some extreme reactions similar to boiling the upper atmosphere. People in the Southwest U.S. have observed what appears to be an auroral effect similar to the Northern Lights, usually only seen in the extreme north. No one has been able to explain this effect.

Hoagland and Begich also feel that the government is using high altitude observation with infrared cameras to discover the location of hidden information about ancient societies. Hoagland feels that this information is buried at the South Pole and that the U.S. Government is aware that this information has great military value. There might also be information about health that would allow for giving us life spans of 150 to 200 years. With satellites and HAARP, the government can prospect the land mass for evidence. Metaphysical and spiritual people have long known that the Egyptian pyramids and the areas around them hold very important information about how we can move into a New Millennium. The governments are aware of this and want this information.

Listening to sources such as Hoagland and Begich talk about secret black projects and publicized projects that misfire, the big picture tells us that a shift is coming. Few people know about HAARP in Alaska so there is very little opposition to it, yet it will potentially disrupt the electrical balance of the atmosphere.

Another example, according to Hoagland was the space shuttle flight in March 1996 which was intended to release a tethered satellite supposed to generate 3,500 volts with a current of just a few amps. However, it generated over 100,000 volts and over 200 amps, literally burning the tether off where it connected to the shuttle. If it had broken at the satellite end, the tether could have sprung back to hit the space shuttle, destroying it and electrocuting the crew.

The satellite continues to orbit Earth, generating a huge voltage difference along the tether. At night, it is clearly visible to the naked eye. Furthermore, Hoagland and Begich both feel that two airline crashes on the 19th parallel were caused by the backlash of the energy released when the satellite tether broke.

Everything that is out of context with truth and ethics will start to be exposed, malfunction, or be destroyed. Enough scientists currently oppose and expose these black projects that governments will not be able to achieve their objective. The Internet has become such an effective tool to disseminate information around the world that concerned governments are setting up super-computers to monitor the Internet. Again, another sign of the approaching critical mass in consciousness.

Paul Solomon, a teacher I studied with from 1978-84, once told me about a man in Israel by the name of John Pineal who has the keys to the information locked in the pyramid area. There is only one catch. He cannot use the keys until the world is ready to use the information for peaceful purposes. The fact that our governments seek this information for military purposes reveals that we are obviously are not ready to receive it.

It is my feedback and my feeling that we can change the course of the future if we get the message out. "Doom and gloom" predictions abound because, prior to 1994, we didn't know that consciousness could change things. We were headed for the same disastrous end as Atlantis. The power brokers were driving this planet to destruction and a possible burnout, impelled by fear of loss of power and control. But we can never get enough power to overcome our fear and make us feel secure.

Trying to overcome fear by clamoring for more control becomes an addiction that will never end because our greed will never be satisfied. The addiction for power is so rampant on this planet that people do anything to grasp power. But those with addictions eventually breakdown due to the stress of having to run ever farther and faster to keep ahead of the addiction. In the end, we never get enough of what we crave, so striving for power is ultimately self-defeating. That is why societies, countries and governments have failed in the past.

Art Bell, one of the loudest voices in the field of "whistle-blowing," was silenced early in the morning of October 13, 1998. At 2:55 a.m., Art announced to his listening audience that he was quitting his talk radio show "for reasons I cannot divulge at the present time." Art's audience is made up largely of conspiracy theory buffs, and the Internet was immediately abuzz with theories about "who got to Art?" Speculation ran rampant with stories such as the one about Single Seven, a time-traveler from the future, coming back to warn Art of an impending situation in which Art's wife would die.

Whether Art Bell is silenced for ever or just temporarily, enough of us now have gotten the message, and we are disseminating it at a phenomenal rate. Not only that but people from all walks of life are getting the message, too. The Hundredth Monkey Theory is working. Those of us who realize that personal power is not power over others are able to take our power back. We are recognizing that we have to cooperate, not compete.

Expect to see major shifts in government, scientific and medical communities from 1999 on. The landslide is already starting to happen. This exponential growth will reach critical mass quickly. There is so much scientific material surfacing now that one has to question: how long can they keep it covert?

[1] High Energy Active Auroral Project uses a phased array of large-dish transmitter/receivers to pump enormous energy into the ionosphere to see what the effects will be. The signal can be tightly focused to disrupt the airspace over a country or region, knocking out radio communication and disturbing the weather. Depending on the frequencies used, it could also cause psychological disruption among the population.

10

The Philadelphia Experiment

IN 1943, THE WAR WAS taking a heavy toll on U.S. warships in the Pacific and Atlantic Oceans, and the U.S. Navy was conducting an ultra-top-secret experiment to make ships invisible to enemy radar. The intent was to create an "electromagnetic bottle" around a ship to deflect radar. Due to over-zealous Navy personnel, the experiment was being pushed faster than was safe, an act that was to have disastrous consequences for the crew of the Navy cruiser involved. As the story unfolds, we'll meet the chief participants: two brothers, Duncan and Edward Cameron, one of whom would later come to be known as Al Bielek.

At a Seattle conference in September, 1995, I had dinner with Al Bielek. I felt it had been an enlightening night of conversation and I thought no more about it. However, my mind did not drop it. That night my subconscious, catalyzed by the meeting, was digging up old memories. This has happened many times in my life; I simply go back, review my dreams, and more information surfaces, which usually proves to be accurate. This time was no exception. What emerged started Al and I on a wild detective chase into perhaps the most fascinating phenomenon in this country's history.

I was born in 1919 in Seattle and joined the Navy in 1940 immediately on graduating from college with a degree in electrical engineering. I was commissioned and posted to a ship in the Philadelphia area. As I dug deeper in my research, I found that in 1943 I had been a junior officer on the cruiser USS Eldridge, the focus of the Philadelphia Experiment. When I'd heard about the project, I'd eagerly volunteered for it. (Why I didn't remember this will become apparent.)

97

The intent of the experiment was to render a ship invisible to the enemy during World War II. The technology was based on two decades of theoretical study into invisibility at Princeton. The equipment used was based on Tesla transformer and generator technology to develop an electrical field that would divert radar signals and even light waves around the ship. The first test in 1940 at the Brooklyn Naval Yard was successful. Using generators on other ships, a small Navy tender was made invisible to the naked eye, yet curiously, the depression in the water left from the boat was clearly visible.

By 1941, we were ready to use shipboard generators, but Tesla wanted more time to prepare because of danger to personnel from being on the same ship as such high-powered generators and high frequency energy. However, the war was going badly and the Navy was unwilling to delay. Tesla left the project amidst rumors that he'd sabotaged it to justify his dropping out. (Although there is no evidence of foul play, many feel that the government had a part in Tesla's death in January, 1943. Why his body was cremated the day after his death has never been explained. Yet other rumors have him secretly relocated by the government to England.)

John Von Neumann of the Institute for Advanced Studies, a mathematical genius of the same caliber as Tesla and Einstein, took over the project. (He was later to join the team that developed the first computer in 1946.) Von Neumann wanted a special ship equipped for the test. The USS Eldridge was selected and rigged with massive degaussing coils and generators for the test scheduled for July 20, 1943 at Philadelphia Naval Yard.

The Cameron brothers operated the generators, and the first test began without problems but was halted after 15 minutes because, again, the depression in the water was inexplicably larger than the ship and the crew was immediately nauseous and disoriented. Edward and Duncan Cameron felt that something was very wrong.

For the second test on August 12, 1943, the strength of the electromagnetic field from onboard generators was increased dramatically by adding a third generator, but due to insufficient testing, it was not synchronized with the other two. Everything went well for about five minutes but then the experiment went completely out of control. The Cameron brothers tried to abort the test but couldn't turn the generators off.

The Eldridge disappeared for four hours from the Philadelphia Naval Yard and was seen in Norfolk, VA. When it rematerialized in Philadelphia, the horrifying toll on the crew became apparent. Many of them had simply disappeared and three were embedded into the superstructure of the ship, dying in agony, literally out of their minds. The remaining survivors were incoherently insane. What outside observers didn't know was that the field strength had been so high that it had actually pushed the ship into another dimension. Being in the shielded generator room saved the Cameron brothers who lived to tell their story.

Unknown in the 1940s was that research over the next 40 years would reveal that the planet undergoes many cycles, with one particular cycle peaking on August 12 every 20 years. On August 12, 1983, experimenters at the top-secret Montauk Air Force facility on Long Island knew this and were waiting for the Philadelphia Experiment test of August 12, 1943. (They had been running their generators nonstop since August 5.) Their intent was to link generated fields across the 40-year span to create a vortex that would pull the Eldridge into a dimensional shift. It worked and the Eldridge was relocated a distance of 400 miles.

Duncan Cameron reported that he and Edward had jumped overboard and, unlike the Eldridge, had materialized at the Montauk facility on August 12, 1983. He described his experience as very bizarre because he saw modern inventions such as helicopters and couldn't figure out what they were. (In 1943, helicopters had not been developed.)

They were escorted to the basement of a building and debriefed. by a much older John Von Neumann. Von Neumann informed them that this was 1983, forty years into their future. He gave them a tour of what was then called the Phoenix Project. He told them that the reason they couldn't turn the Eldridge's generators off was that they had locked with the Montauk generators. Apparently they were still running and, due to the locked fields, the Montauk technicians couldn't shut off their equipment either. The only solution was to have the Camerons return to the ship to stop the equipment. Von Neumann reassured them that history recorded that they had succeeded, and that they should even destroy the equipment if necessary.

The Cameron brothers returned to the ship and destroyed the generators, thus ending the test and returning the Eldridge to Philadelphia. However, just before the dimensional portal closed, Duncan returned to 1983 Montauk while Edward remained in 1943 Philadelphia. Why Duncan did this has never been revealed. His body began to age very quickly, and an odd request was made of Duncan's father. Montauk reached back in time from 1983 to 1947 and asked Duncan Sr. to quickly father another son into whose body the soul of Duncan Jr. could be transferred. (Apparently the Montauk facility had developed such technology.)

Duncan Cameron Sr. was a mysterious shadowy figure in the experiment, and his role has never been revealed. Speculation hints that he was somehow involved in smuggling scientists who disagreed with the methods of the Third Reich from Germany to the United States.

Duncan Sr. complied, and by 1952, Duncan Jr. had a younger brother, also named Duncan. The boy was nine years old when, on August 12, 1963, the 20-year cycle once again peaked, and Duncan's soul was transferred to the young boy. So the original brothers were now separated by 20 years, but to Edward, his brother had disappeared and would not reappear into his life until 1963!

Meanwhile, Edward continued his Navy career, but became too outspoken for the top brass. His memory was somehow wiped clean and he was age-regressed back in time as the son of a couple who had just lost their young son, a Mr. and Mrs. Bielek. They named their new son Al, and he has gone by that name since. Al grew up normally, became an engineer, and ironically, went to work at Montauk. He could remember nothing about his experiences until 1988, when his memory started returning. He now remembers that he was born as Edward Cameron. He left Montauk and dedicates his life to private research and speaking publicly about his experiences.

To return to the Philadelphia Experiment, four of the crew that jumped overboard underwent a different experience. They were caught in a "side tunnel" of the portal and materialized in 1978 near Four Corners at the Arizona, Colorado, Utah and New Mexico borders where a portal between dimensions exists.. By jumping ship, they had "bi-located," or duplicated with one version trapped in the future and the other returning to 1943 with the Eldridge.

My conversation with Al Bielek spawned many dreams and past life recall about the experiment. I felt that this was something I should pursue to discover what my inner self was trying to reveal to me. The more I investigated this situation, the more I began to recall about my experiences. Further evaluation and regression work revealed that I was one of the four. At dinner, I found that the same information was coming back to Al, having been suppressed by some form of mind control when the Navy decided to eliminate Edward Cameron.

I did not return with the ship because I missed the time portal since I was in the future when the ship returned to 1943. Al Beilek ended up at Montauk. Since he was in the future he was not aware that he could get back. He was informed in that future that they had the ability to send him back to the ship to stop the experiment. He went back, but since I didn't have access to the time travel equipment, I couldn't go back. So I was locked into the future.

In 1978, I lived in dual time-space with the 35-year time displacement for eighteen months. The "me" that returned experienced a form of "double vision" that allowed me to see a person as they were in 1943 and an overlay of how they would look in 1978. For some reason, I was able to deal with the disorientation, but two of my shipmates couldn't and died shortly afterwards. The third disappeared and I lost track of him, making me the only known survivor of the 1943/1978 time shift. This curious experience on February 23, 1945 ended with the death of the "me" that had jumped into the future.

By 1980, I had concluded that the only way I could reconcile the two timelines and end the duality disorientation was to let the "me" who had jumped into the future die. Then the "me" that had aged naturally would no longer be caught in the time paradox. That "me" could then go back from 1980 and return to 1945 where I would die (apparently from the effects of the experiment) and walk into another body. That would end the paradox once and for all.

For 32 days, I was out-of-body while I negotiated with the Lords of Karma and the soul of a young boy named Art Martin who was eight years old (in 1945). Young Art was having a terrible time and wanted to die. He was in a coma, having engineered an illness that no one would suspect as suicide (see Chapter 11 for more details). Art left his body on March 25, 1945, and I walked into it, having left my body on February 23, 1945. Of course, I appeared to die on that date, apparently a belated victim of the ill-fated Philadelphia Experiment. I quickly pulled Art's body out of the coma, healed the damage completely, and, to the astonishment of the doctors, left the hospital three days later.

Once I was focused solely in the 1940s timeline, the next 23 years (1945 – 1978) included many strange phenomena such as out-of-body experiences in which I would be on the ceiling looking down at my body. These were triggered by having a parallel life in the future. I tried discussing this, I was met with a number of responses, none of them the least bit supportive.

Encountering the year 1978 for the second time, there were now two of me once again co-existing in the same time-frame. The parallel lifetimes caused me to blank out at times and I had no control over when would happen. I tried to leave that parallel existence in 1978 but was unsuccessful since I hadn't put all the pieces together at that time.

Then began the lengthy process of dealing with the young Art's body karma detailed in Chapter 11. As Art Martin, the weird experiences continue to this day. For example, things often simply disappear into other dimensions and may or may not return to the same place. My pager, for example, has disappeared five times and usually reappears at the paging company office, which costs me $25.00 for the reward fee. But no one can tell me who got the reward because no one knows how the pager got there. One time, I left it in a friend's house and it reappeared two days later at the video counter in the local supermarket a mile away. This is often frustrating because I lose things I need and have to replace them or do without. Once, I went to get some printing done and left my Daytimer at the store counter. Returning 45 minutes later, it was missing. It turned up two weeks later next to one of cash registers and the manager found it when she opened the store up one morning.

By 1996, this dual parallel life situation was getting out of hand so we went back to see what we could do to clear it up. With a future portal open, events were happening to me that I could neither explain or understand. For example, I was in two single-car wrecks because I had blacked out. Another time, I ran a red light and clipped off the front of another car. Fortunately, there was minimal damage to both vehicles. I would sit down at my computer to write and in a few minutes, I would pass out. Obviously something was trying to stop me from writing my books.

We found that I was in denial that I had anything to write about, even though I knew I had much to say. On the other hand, certain aliens and demons were helping to push me out of my body so that

I couldn't write. Other times, I would just walk out of my body and later have no idea where I went. It seemed that I would walk out of my body and go into this other lifetime. We finally traced the programs in my mind that were causing the situation. Apparently, a sub-personality was very upset that I lost all the knowledge from that lifetime. It also saw me as more successful in that lifetime and with more prestige so it wanted to return to that lifetime. We finally cleared all the programs and reunited all my sub-personalities into one me. We also erased, deleted and destroyed all the operating systems that were driving that parallel life time and closed the portal that was causing all the problems. Everything is now quiet on the western front.

The Philadelphia Experiment caused a major breach in an inter-dimensional portal, which in turn created an opening for negative extraterrestrials to enter at will. Hence the rash of UFO sightings in the late 1940s to early 1980s.

Apparently, three UFOs appeared over the USS Eldridge on August 5, 1943 and hovered until the fateful day of August 12. When the switch was thrown, two of them made a quick getaway, but the third was sucked into the vortex, rematerializing deep underground at Montauk. The Cameron brothers were reportedly involved in recovering sensitive technology from the UFO that the ETs didn't want the U.S. to have at that time.

With this portal open until 1983, the U.S. Government had no choice except to make a deal with the aliens, so they concluded a contract in 1954. Unfortunately, the government negotiators did not understand that these extraterrestrials were Dark Forces of the alien world. We paid dearly for that ignorance. They infiltrated all of our technical schools and research facilities, and as a result, we now have many problems in trying to create peace on this planet.

As a footnote, on August 27, 1996, my colleagues and I finally forced the Orions to pull out. On September 7, 1996, we discovered a small band of rebellious Pleiadians with an Orion computer trying to slip back in. With information from the Intergalactic Council, we managed to force them out, too. With all the Dark Force aliens removed from the planet, the way is paved for a major breakthrough in the transformation of this planet.

I have formed an open research project to support this work into the future, adding the information in successive editions.

I seek dedicated volunteers to help us in our quest to move consciousness to critical mass so we can make this quantum leap into the Fifth Dimension.

11

Neuro/Cellular Repatterning

S OMEDAY IN THE FUTURE, ALL practitioners no matter what their specialty will recognize that the body/mind is a *hologram*. Medical science believes that we can control pain and disease by suppressing the symptom with drugs, or by manipulating or removing the offending part of the body to heal it. But what affects one part also affects the whole. Body, mind, and spirit interact to form an integrated, functioning entity.

If you give yourself love and a feeling of "rightness," the body will heal itself through the power of the mind. God created a perfect body and included directions and lessons on how to have an abundant, happy, healthy life, yet we lost track of the directions. When we decided we know more about the process of healing and recovery than God, we separated from God and the inherent healing power of the mind through God. This is Universal Law.

Judgment, self-righteousness and self-rejection impair the natural healing. Anger and fear cause only contraction and more pain. Love, forgiveness, and acceptance cause happiness, expansion, and healing. The mind's programming is the base cause of all physical discomfort. With the knowledge offered here, people can make accurate choices to heal illness, disease, addictions, dysfunctional relationships, and fear of intimacy without damage or pain to their body and mind. When we understand that there is no lack of love, we can heal our separation from God. We can heal anything with love. Recovery is possible, miracles do happen. All you have to do is step out of illusion and denial.

We dedicate this work to give people a true understanding of the responsibility, to owning own personal power, and to telling the truth. Love, peace, happiness, joy, and harmony are our right and inheritance. We can have it all right now once we let go of control, and anything we truly let go of will come back to us ten-fold.

Understanding Dis-ease

Healing is a process brought about by releasing the programs and core beliefs that drive your life. There is no disease, illness or dysfunctional behavior that just comes on and affects us by happenstance. Your mind controls all actions you take and all situations that happen to you. Bacteria, viruses, and fungi do not *cause* disease. They are the result of a breakdown in your body's immune system, again caused by the mind. We would like to blame our problems on someone else or a disease going around but it doesn't work like that. My children were exposed to many contagious diseases growing up but were never were affected by them. Health is a matter of how you feel about yourself.

We set everything up to get a certain payoff. Quite often we have no knowledge as to why we set it up or how to get out of the situation. In fact most of the time, we are so far into illusion that we cannot even understand why or how we ended up with whatever we have afflicting us. Our first thought is that it is physical: you can feel the pain, but pain is just a signal that something needs to be heard. Pain is also resistance to locating the cause. Rather than locating the cause at the mental and emotional levels, we run to the doctor for drugs to control the symptom. Anything that removes pain or discomfort without addressing the cause is just sidestepping the issue.

The base cause is what happened to cause you to react in the beginning. How you respond or react to the catalyst will govern how it affects you. Your interpretation will either set up a belief or a program. Each time you run into the same catalyst you will react, based on the program or belief. Over time, your programs and beliefs become established patterns that cause you react in the same manner each time, thus reinforcing the pattern even further. However, it may be many years before enough charge builds up to cause an illness.

The payoff for all illness and disease is getting attention and approval. We will do anything to get a concentrated form of attention. Our motivation is to find someone who will provide the attention we need. We may not call it love, but that is how our mind interprets it. Children get sick to get attention. If they get enough love and acceptance, they do not get sick.

Conditional love comes in many forms. It could be abuse at any level, even physical. How we view love depends on how we were treated as children. True love is acceptance without judgment. It is kindness and caring without any put downs or attempts to control or manipulate. Using parental authority to control behavior is also conditional love. If you were never picked up and hugged, or never got a pat on the back as a child, you grew up not knowing what approval is. As a result, you may grow up without a basic unconditional love program. Without this program, most people get sick very often as their body/mind tries to get someone, anyone to give them attention.

Most people are unable to accept love at a deep level of their being. We cannot get approval and acceptance from others until we are able to give it to ourselves. As long as we feel others should give love to us, it will not be unconditional. Almost everyone has a hook or a cord connected to their need for support or help. Many people will seek out and find someone that they can cling to in an effort to get attention. So for healing to take place, we must release all the rejection and abandonment we have received throughout our lives.

We will do anything to get recognition. It is the basic desire of all people to be recognized and validated. Sickness is one of the ploys we use to cause someone to recognize that we are alive. Total rejection will cause death, because if you think you're not wanted, why be here? HIV and AIDS are examples of the result of total rejection. Society does not accept you, so you reject yourself. Most diseases are caused by selective immunity, but with AIDS, the immune system breaks down totally, so there's no protection from disease. When the T-cell count drops to a level where the body cannot attack bacteria and viruses, they will flourish and grow.

How, then, do we resolve the dilemma? Through unconditional love. That is all that will heal the body permanently. To achieve this end, we must remove all the programs, patterns, and records from the subconscious and conscious mind that are precursors to disease and illness.

Patterns and Programs

The encrypted and encoded programs stored within the body are the most damaging because they existed before you were born. They can destroy your self-esteem, self-worth, self-confidence, and your validation of self. If you feel you have no value, you will continually choose people in your life who will invalidate your credibility as a person. Bonding with your mother at birth is very important. Your relationship with primary caregivers and how they treated you as a child will control the balance of your life. How you interpreted the way people treated you set up lifelong patterns, and most people reject themselves based on this childhood programming.

The power of your mind is awesome. It will actually stop drugs, herbs, minerals, vitamins, or any useful products from being assimilated by the body if the programs and beliefs are intent on rejecting the body. It may allow selective acceptance if you make a commitment to taking care of your health. This is why many nutritional therapies work so well. They give the body adjuncts to help it clear the toxic materials that have been deposited so it will begin to heal. You can also use electronic instruments that will remove pain by allowing the body's electrical functions return to normal. Many alternative therapies will adjust the body through manipulation or energy transfer but, if you do not get to the base cause and remove the program, the same condition will return.

When we review this information objectively without prejudice we can clearly see that illness and disease are a state of mind. They only exist in the body because of the beliefs, concepts, patterns and programs that are driving them. In actuality, illness and disease do not exist. There are contagious people who have programs, patterns, beliefs, interpretations and concepts about illness and disease that cause them to be subject to dysfunctional beliefs that allow them to accept physical breakdown.

In my case I have not seen a doctor in over twenty years. My only sickness in the last 28 years was caused by working too many days without time off, combined with pressure from emotional release and extreme stress. It only took a few days to recover when I realized what I had done to myself.

The challenge is: *you must be able to recognize the symptom and what your body is saying to you.* Very few people can read their own book very well, so the records are not accessible. Doctors will tell you that you have no recourse and that your body will continue to degenerate, and that is the way it is. Meanwhile, the body is building up defenses to drugs because it wants you to get the message.

All we have to do is rewrite scripts by reprogramming the mind. It's very simple to do when you have access to the records. Suppose the pattern is coming out of a past life. If so, you will have to release the karmic contracts and agreements you made that follow you everywhere you go, lifetime after lifetime. You cannot talk them out; they must be removed from cellular memory. Miracles happen when you clear and release them.

To understand the theory of healing you have to understand that nobody can heal you. You have to do it yourself. The Catch 22 is: You must be willing to release yourself from the past programming without blame, justification, or judgment.

Throughout my books, you will find the statement. "You must take your power back, reclaim your personal power, and take responsibility." Making a commitment and sticking to it with discipline is hard for most people. They will confront the issues, then turn and run. The most common problem in our society is denial based on the illusion: "My life is all right the way it is."

When we get life in order, healing happens at cellular mind level. We do not have to project our anger and fear onto other people but can respond with unconditional love and forgiveness. We can make friends with our disowned self.

Does Your Body Tell the Truth?

Your body will always tell you the truth if you can get past the facades, masks, fronts, and masquerades set up by your ego, survival self, critical parent and the myriad other sub-personalities in order to block release of this information. If you are willing to step from behind the illusion and denial, it is very easy.

The internal dialogue with yourself is on 24 hours a day, every day of your life. All five senses are continually recording the incidents of your life exactly as they happen, both from outside and from your own thoughts. The brain instantly sorts the input and sends it to the proper area of your mind. Each cell has a memory that records all your thoughts with chemical and micro-electrical impulses. Negative thoughtform inputs will cause physical and mental/emotional changes. As they build up, they will begin to organize into dysfunctional patterns in your mind and body. This cellular memory will continue to build on the existing programs, etching the pattern deeper and deeper until it is released.

Pain, emotional, mental or physical, is just a symptom of resistance. You cannot release the symptoms and expect healing to happen. You must access the base cause and the core issues that created the pain in the first place.

To understand how your mind has recorded events in your life, we use kinesiology and intuitive listening to let the subconscious mind talk to us. It will give us the dialogue just as it happened. You can identify the person, the age, and the specific program created by the incident. An affirmation specifically tailored to the situation will release the pattern and program.

We are not interested in the obvious displayed symptom, but the actual cause that is disrupting the body/mind function. The outward symptom is very seldom the core issue. It is almost always caused by a false belief or a misinterpretation held in the subconscious mind. If a client is open to any possibility, we can locate and release the core issue causing the breakdown in the body/mind. There is no need to explore the symptoms or make a diagnosis. The dysfunction will heal itself once we release the core issue, usually caused by rejection, fear, anger, validation, or lack of love.

To change the dysfunctional behavior pattern, we must locate the record and the program in the body/mind from childhood or past lives. To release the walls and barriers we set up to block ourselves from others' love and who we are, cellular memory must be released. This frees you from delusion and denial to receive the basic needs of all people: self-love, validation, and a deep sense of "I'm okay."

Without these three basic human needs, achieving self-worth, self-esteem, acceptance, and approval is difficult. Our basic need is to give and receive love—the only power that heals. Depending how we react to a situation, we are in one of three states: love, fear, or the transition from one to the other. There is no gray area; it is love or fear.

Each time you hold or accept any attack thought or action, you have accepted the specific programming into your body/mind. Disapproval, rejection, and abandonment have a strong emotional and physical effect on you. Your body will tell the truth if you listen and let it reveal what's causing the dysfunction.

Emotional pain is non-tangible and can be denied or covered up, yet it can be as debilitating as physical pain. However, if we can forgive and love the person or situation, it is released. When you release the destructive instructions in your mind, you can claim your personal power, self-esteem, and self worth. *There is no lack of love in God's world*, yet many people shut themselves off from it. All we have to do step out of illusion and denial and open the door with forgiveness, recognizing that love is our inheritance. Miracles happen when you step out of denial.

Not a therapist alive can heal you. Only *you* can heal you. You must heal yourself. But you must first commit to confronting your denial and illusion. When you accept the challenge to be vulnerable and to take responsibility, healing is possible.

Many people feel that they are already taking full responsibility in their life. But if we interpret responsibility as the "ability to respond," can they respond to any situation with kindness and caring, without any justification, anger, or the need to control? If they can respond in every situation without feeling fear and/or rejection, and understand that they create every incident in their lives without blame, they will experience instantaneous transformation.

My Journey to Freedom: the Birth of N/CR

As a child, I was different from other children. I knew about things before they happened. When a school class bored me, I would go to sleep and get sent to the nurse to take a nap. I would come back to class, take a test on a topic I missed, and get a perfect score. I did not study much yet got above average grades. I was a rebel who would do as I wanted. Subjects in which I was interested came easily, yet I would fail subjects in which I had no interest and didn't care if I failed. I always wondered why.

When I tried hypnotic regression to go back to my early childhood, I couldn't get any answers or visual experiences before the age of ten. I was puzzled why, as an adult, I had no memory of childhood until I discovered during a Dick Sutphen seminar that I walked-in at the age of eight. But why did my memory cut off at age ten?

After lengthy discussions with my mother, we pieced together why the original soul in my body wanted out. At age eight, he could no longer deal with the trauma of his life and set up a drama in which he could kill himself without it looking like suicide. The doctors misdiagnosed a ruptured intestine as stomach flu and the complications from the poisons draining into the body gave him a one-in-ten chance of living. He was in a coma for six days at which point I took over the body. The doctors said I would be in the hospital for six to eight weeks but I left the hospital totally healed in three days. The doctors were totally confounded; all they could say was "miracles do happen." They were unaware that a new soul who didn't have the karmic programs had taken over the body. They couldn't understand what had happened, nor could they have dealt with it.

His mother had not wanted children so he was rejected before birth. She tried to abort him unsuccessfully. If she had to have a child, she wanted a girl, so, until I entered the body, he got treated much like a girl. He was an introverted loner with almost no friends. He was left-handed and the school teachers convinced his mother they could force him to use his right hand. This caused right/left brain confusion with bi-cameral integration trauma resulting in total dyslexia. He could not keep up with the other students because the writing in the school books appeared backward on the page. He wrote from right to left, so his writing could only be read in a mirror. As a result, the school system planned to put him in a disabled learning class.

To the outside world, his mother appeared to be very supportive; on the inside, she covertly manipulated him to make him feel unwanted. When he was six, his father gave him a beautiful tricycle for Christmas. It was a rebuilt second-hand tricycle because you couldn't get metal toys during the war. After about three months, his mother put it in the basement and locked it up saying that he was not taking care of it, when all he was doing was letting other children ride it. She said that children who didn't have toys wouldn't take care of them and would destroy his tricycle. This happened twice according to his mother. The third time, she sold it. How can a six-year-old understand that his mother sold his most prized possession to teach him a lesson?

To her dying day, she claimed she did the right thing. This experience destroyed his self-worth and self-esteem; he felt he had no value. Probing more deeply, we discovered his mother was not really angry with him at all. The tricycle represented his father, and his father had made a bond with him through the tricycle which angered her.

When he was seven years old, his parents had marital problems and his mother moved out, abandoning him. His father had to structure his day to get him to school and arrange to pick him up. But in 1943, the schools couldn't handle disabled-learning children so he was put in a regular class and couldn't keep up. This must have been the last straw; the fatal illness accident occurred six months later. Of course, all this happened well below his conscious awareness.

At the soul level, I knew that this family would provide me with what I needed to accelerate my growth and that I would have to take on the karma that was locked into the body. Clearing his "body" karma took me ten years. By age 18, it felt good to be my own person but that feeling was just another illusion because the major lessons were yet to come. It would take another 22 years to get on the path.

To continue the story, my mother resented my father and verbally abused him. She was a passive/aggressive personality and my father gave his power away to her all the time. He finally gave up after overcoming four life-threatening diseases. His only escape was to leave the body. My interpretation was that my father was the problem. He had an extreme inferiority complex, and mother played right into it.

The movie, *Field of Dreams*, was a catalyst for me to get my feelings out about my father. The second time I saw it, about three-quarters through, I started crying and could not stop. It took more than 30 minutes of processing to clear it. It apparently brought out all the feelings I had repressed. For the next six months, whenever a sensitive situation came up in a client session that was similar to my experience, I would start crying during the session. I finally realized that my father was a good father; he did the best he could. He did everything for me he could.

Some parents felt I was spoiled. Many children asked if I would trade parents with them. My parents were a "typical John Bradshaw couple" who couldn't express love. They thought that doing things for me and giving me physical objects expressed love. I finally realized, 15 years after his death, how good my father really was to me. If I'd been aware of the situation at the time, I would have practiced considerable forgiveness to release myself from the misplaced anger that I had. And he would have probably lived much longer.

Fear of female domination was locked into my family to the point that, until I was 18, I was afraid of girls. All of my early programming told me that I was not all right, to the point that I would go out of my way to create situations that would validate my "rejection" feelings. Until I was 57 years old, if I was offered the choice between something that was perfect and something defective, I would choose the defective product.

The fact that my soul took over this body told me that I obviously needed to deal with these inherited programs. I'd had no prior lives with my parents, so I knew there were no lessons there.

I was so locked into my mother that I would put myself at risk financially to get love from her. Her form of love was giving me money. So my way to get love was to get into a financial bind so I had to ask her for money. It was very humiliating to have to ask for money and be asked, "Why can't you handle your money better?" I could make large sums of money on investments and business but I could not hold onto it. Something always came up to cause me to give it away. I have since overcome the programs and am starting to recover financially.

Between ages of 30 and 40 I shrank a full inch To deal with this and other physical conditions, I consulted medical doctors, but they could find no physical reason. I had a double "S" curve in my spine, along with degeneration at specific points which doctors could not understand. That only happened to people with osteoporosis which I didn't have because my bones were strong. However, they were actually being eaten away. I had such intense sciatic pain that I would double up and had to sit down. I was told that at the rate my body was breaking down, I would soon end up in a wheelchair. Today, there is no evidence of the debilitating 24-hour-a-day pain of 20 years ago. The fact that I have since run five marathons of over 26 miles proves to me the awesome power of the mind.

Two teachers, Beesley and Solomon, showed me the way out. When I found a way, I went for it. I spent all my time working through the jungle of feelings and emotional trauma. In 1982, with my newfound awareness, I set up a therapy practice but found that talk therapy does not get to the cause. I developed my own program, which I titled "Body/Mind Integration," and later "Cellular Repatterning" because we were releasing the imbedded cellular memory from past experiences.

Each cell remembers its blueprint—the perfect image of how it can regenerate itself. If there is no dysfunctional negative emotional energy blocking cellular structures, they will regenerate perfectly from their blueprints each time the cells are rebuilt. I added the "Neuro" prefix in 1988 when I discovered that we were erasing the pattern used by the neurological system to keep muscles in trauma from past negative emotional experiences.

When I first discovered N/CR, it was difficult to define the process. For 25 years, I'd sought a cure for my own physical problems by sampling all the alternatives to allopathic medicine. Not one person could understand my problem or alleviate my pain. I thought nutrition might be the key, but it was only part of the solution. When I discovered the power of the mind, I realized it was not what you put in your mouth that is important, but what your mind accepts as truth. I then looked for a process that could get to the base cause of dysfunction without having to spend hours trying to dig the cause out of a client who doesn't understand it in the first place. Most people don't even know what their mind has stored, let alone understand it. Initially, I failed to connect my physical pain with emotional dysfunction within the programs in my mind. I thought all physical problems had only physical origins; at least that's what doctors told me. Yet they did not understand why my spine was deteriorating. I was given an ultimate prognosis of wheelchair, but no specified cause.

I decided psychology might have the answer, but it seemed to me that conventional psychology tried to fix blame on someone or something unknown. I did not believe we had to be victims of another person's reaction. At the time, I didn't know that my body was continually dialoging with me; if I listened, it would reveal the causes. In my training with Paul Solomon, I approached psychology from a holistic, spiritual aspect, a very different slant from my original training. It did answer some of my questions and helped me understand the dialogue but it did not heal my body. Ronald Beesley, in a workshop, showed me how the body stores the memory and the basics of removing it. This knowledge gave me the tools to integrate spiritual psychology with body/mind therapy. This became the link which I incorporated as the basis of N/CR and my counseling.

Neuro/Cellular Repatterning (N/CR) works with the subconscious mind to help reprogram the dysfunctional programs and behavior patterns. Occasionally with N/CR, the ego or subconscious programming will try to block but with biofeedback, we can access any program or pattern in the body/mind.

In 1994, I was introduced to a new way of using biofeedback instruments by Dr. John Craig. Biofeedback is typically seen as a way to train yourself to handle stress or learn how to control the body's reactions. This again is symptomatic treatment, because you are controlling the result. You are the victim of the stress until you locate the core issue and release the cause. If you control the effect with behavior modification, it will rise again when you least expect it. Our intention is to get to the base cause and the core issues causing the lack of direction in life, disease, dysfunctional behavior, emotional/ physical pain, anger, fear, or mental/physical discomfort.

NC/R uses biofeedback instruments for a totally different application, akin to a polygraph or lie detector. The difference is that whether clients are telling the truth or not is irrelevant because they seldom know the actual cause. We use a dual channel biofeedback instrument to track the conscious and subconscious minds' responses to the questions we ask. During treatments, the instrument indicates whether the actual behavior pattern was released or whether the ego is blocking the release. Our intention is to locate irrational, illogical, self defeating, destructive and dysfunctional behavior patterns that are locked in the subconscious mind.

The biofeedback instruments proved to be a great help in finally getting my ego to understand that it had a contract with me and that it was fighting a losing battle. If it actually won the battle, it would kill my body and in turn destroy itself. I was able to demonstrate ego that the body/mind created it. Since it did not have any connection with my soul, it could not transcend the body at death. Ego decided that it wanted to continue to live and create a new life with me. We came to a successful conclusion with a win-win for both of us. It finally made a decision to stop the battle for control and power over me.

This process is the next step in breaking the barriers to total personal transformation. If you have not come face to face with your ego yet, it will happen. If your ego is running your life, you have a battle on your hands to reclaim control. (For a more comprehensive description, see *Your Body Tells The Truth*.)

It seemed the more I committed myself to spiritual growth and enlightenment, the more intense the battle for survival became. I was committed to become a good speaker and present my work to the world, but I would sabotage myself over and over again for no obvious reason. I would make myself be late to lectures and workshops. My car would break down with no obvious reason. Engines would blow up for no reason at all. Mechanics could not believe how I could damage an engine so extensively that it was unsalvageable. But I now know that I set it all up. This information came at a price; these mishaps cost me thousands of dollars and a lot of credibility.

Even though I knew that my work was effective for my clients, I continually questioned my own effectiveness. Miracles happened all the time, but I found myself denying that I was doing well. On a conscious level, I knew that N/CR worked, yet I would only occasionally get a workshop together. When I did, they were very successful.

It was not until August, 1995 that we found the encrypted programs that had been locked into the body before I was born. These encrypted patterns govern your life before you're born, setting up your life path without your awareness. Before you entered the body, you knew exactly what you were up against with the lesson you chose. But, of course, once you enter the body, you lose the directions, the curriculum, and the program.

When we cleared all the encrypted programs and the encoded patterns and programs, a miracle happened. My life turned around in just two weeks. I could actually watch myself start to sabotage myself and it would turn around right in front of my eyes. The more we cleared, the easier it was to be successful. Now my life works like clockwork. No matter what wall I have to scale or what obstacle comes before me, it all works out very easily. In fact, just like my life, all my vehicles run very well.

I found myself passing out for no reason in the middle of the day, even when working with clients. People accused me of going to sleep. I was afraid to drive at night; one time, I blacked out and ran off the road, almost destroying the car. We have since found that this was due to possession by many forms of entities committed to kill me. They seemed to come in every form, from aliens to demonic. Seven of them had been with me since I took over this body. Now that I have the ability to clear myself, I can deal with this situation much more easily. I am relatively free from the problem now, coming under attack only when the Dark Forces get angry at me for clearing so many of their buddies and sending them to the Light.

With my knowledge on the subject, I am able to help others. It was never my intention to be involved in exorcism, but I have so much experience now that I am writing a book on this subject.

I have achieved freedom from the excruciating pain in my body and in my life and according to my teacher and my Higher Self, I have finally crested the mountain. I no longer self-sabotage. For example, I left my leather pouch where I keep all my money and wallet at a gas station on Highway 5 in California. When I discovered the loss an hour and a half later, I drove all the way back but the wallet was gone. I canceled all my credit cards and got a new driver's license. However, the wallet was returned four days later by mail including the $150 in cash less $20 to cover the cost of mailing. When your life is aligned with spirit, everything falls into line as it has for me now.

It's All In Your Subconscious

We must break through the belief systems created by illusions, but to accomplish this in a conventional therapy setting is impossible since few clients know the base causes. If they do have some understanding, it is usually inaccurate unless they've done considerable processing. Even then they may not understand denial. It is difficult to get clients to revisit painful feelings that are completely blocked by ego or protective programs. If they can, we find they go back into the *emotion* rather than the *feeling*. Most people see no need to dredge up more pain and generally block negative childhood trauma experiences. We have to break through the belief systems that were created by protective illusions. We can then release them with love and forgiveness.

The key to healing is always stored in the subconscious mind. Illness is caused by rejection of self and lack of love. The challenge is in accessing painful traumatic experiences. If a client cannot remember an incident, how do you access and process the issue? Most people will try to describe what they feel is the cause. However, we tend to block out painful traumatic experiences of the past, and with the trauma so totally blocked, we cannot locate the cause. Many clients have attended seminars and workshops on changing their core beliefs and clearing their emotional trauma and/or have been in therapy for decades with many cathartic releases, yet may have experienced very little change in their emotional/mental behavior.

Are we actually getting to the core issue and releasing it? Doctors will tell patients, "You have to live with your pain," or "We can't do anything for you." That may be their truth based on their training but we do not buy this theory at all. If you can locate the base causes and the core issues, you can heal any body or mind dysfunction. Our documented case histories prove that you can heal any dysfunction of the mind or body *if the client wants to do so.*

Clients will say they want to be healed but unfortunately many do not want to confront the fear of change or give up the payoff they're getting from their dysfunction or disease. If you want to be taken care of, and you have created the dysfunction to achieve that end, making any progress in healing will take major transformation in your belief system. Most people who are stuck in their illusion will deny they are holding themselves back. But to me, it's obvious when clients are stuck or don't want to move past their blocks. They lack the will and desire to take responsibility for overcoming the adversity.

When clients are locked in this truth, we can't reach them. In fact, they may accuse you of trying to replace their illusion with yours. If their illusion is their truth, then your truth is an illusion to them. We cannot instill the will to change. It is next to impossible to change a person's illusion. Each person must choose to claim his or her own personal power. In fact, if you do point out a client's denial, he or she will cling to the addiction even harder. Many times you lose a client or a friend because you are seen as a self-righteous meddler.

With biofeedback instruments, we find that the subconscious mind will respond to any question and validate the response so well that you can pinpoint the exact date of the incident and the age of the person at the time. With appropriate questioning, we can locate any blocked traumatic incident in a person's life. Since we work directly with the subconscious mind, the ego cannot block an indication of resistance and we can watch the biofeedback instrument respond as the trauma or pattern is released.

The skeptics or those unwilling to accept that we can locate and understand the actual programs with N/CR can see the responses and the releases on the biofeedback instruments. Many people work for years *assuming* that they're releasing the blocks, but biofeedback instruments actually show the effect graphically. This is a new adjunct to counseling which has a far-reaching effect for those people who feel they are not getting results from counseling. It is an effective tool for use in healing because it gets to any base cause in a very short time.

It is also an excellent tool to recognize how much control your ego has over you. The ego cannot block the information. You can demonstrate to your ego how to make friends with it. By cutting through its defenses, you let it know where it tries to control. This is one of the few ways I found that you can work on yourself. You can process yourself in an effective manner once you learn how to use the instruments. We feel this is the next step toward facilitating the path to personal transformation and self-healing.

Since 1994, I have become familiar with how the mind responds to the biofeedback instrument. I have developed a method to dialogue with the ego that will get it to release its control and cooperate with you. It is very easy to recognize when the ego is blocking; the withholds, denials and illusions are obvious. We know when we have released the core issue and can get fast, successful results.

How Body Cells Communicate

Today, many renowned speakers stress the importance of love to a healthy body and mind. Ten years ago, they would have been laughed at by the medical community but now professionals in the medical field are actually making these claims. Medical researchers are now discovering that the body communicates positive or negative impulses to itself through chemicals such as neuropeptides (NPs). At one time, it was thought that only the brain released NPs but now it is clear that all cells communicate with NPs.

NPs are like the acid in a car battery. When you turn on the car ignition, a chemical reaction in the battery releases electrical energy. In the same way, NPs release minute electrical impulses that tell the various parts of your body what to do. Thus the neurological system operates on electrical impulses. A message of fear or anger creates a response that is destructive in your body. However, the body doesn't interpret it as, "this is a dysfunctional message." It does exactly what your mind instructs it to do. Our basic need is to give and receive love, so a loving state sends a healing, loving message to the body.

Why can't researchers can find a cure for disease? Because disease is created by the mind's communication with the cellular structure. You cannot remove a pattern from the mind by removing the dysfunctional part of the body. The program is still functional, so the disease will be created again and again until the body dies or the dysfunctional program is released. Conversely, you cannot remove emotional pain by going through a cathartic release. It may release the pent-up anger or fear, but it will not remove the program. No amount of affirmations on, say, forgiving and releasing a person will work if you do not release the program that caused the emotional pain. The pain will return again and again until it is released from the physical body/mind.

Pain indicates resistance; 15 years of experience has shown that all we need do is decipher the message causing the pain, and we can release the dysfunction. Then the original programs can perform as they were intended to. This is why N/CR works so well. We tell the subconscious mind to release and the NPs do the work for us, provided that ego or the middle-self do not try to intervene and stop the process.

Medical research has discovered that each cell has the ability to communicate. But doctors are baffled when drugs and surgery have only selective success on disease. We can work with people with whom the medical practitioner has given up and we can trigger healing. We don't diagnose or use drugs; all we need do is access the base cause. When we locate the cause (who, when, why, and how you reacted to the stimuli), we rewrite the program and treat it with the most important ingredients—self-love, forgiveness, self-acceptance, and validation.

The Body/Mind: A Vehicle for Personal Transformation

Everyone would like to live in happiness, joy, harmony, and unconditional love. So why do we continue to follow the same path if it doesn't bring us joy? Because the illusion we live in denies the truth. So we exist in the illusion unaware that there's another path.

Most of the time, we feel that if we have the concept down and the goal clearly in our mind, we can accomplish the task. Most clients put honest effort into changing their attitudes and behavior in order to reclaim their self-esteem and self-worth. but many seem unable to accomplish their goal and become discouraged, frustrated, and disappointed. However, we overlook the fact that our belief systems, coupled with our subconscious mind, are very powerful. The challenge is to get *all* our minds to accept the need for change. Conscious mind must be in alignment with the subconscious and the instinctual minds, or you will be sabotaged.

Dr. Wayne Dyer put it so aptly: you will be unable to see the situation until you can recognize it and believe it. If you suppress or stuff your feelings, an illusion or denial will block your recognition of any situation you are unable to handle. If you deny the threat, it does not exist in your reality. Of course, that does not mean that the situation does not exist. It may just exist separate from your willingness to recognize it.

As newborns, we formed our beliefs according to how we reacted to how our primary caregivers treated us. The programs continue throughout our life, or until we change our beliefs. Young children have very little control over the impact of parents' behavior. We lose our self-esteem and "all-rightness" by giving away our personal power and allowing others to control how we feel. Very few parents realize they are teaching their children negative emotions of rejection, disapproval, scolding, shame, guilt, and fear.

Some children are so sensitive to what is said to them that how they were treated programs their lives failure or success. As a result, they give up control of their personal power and begin to reject themselves before their first birthday. Most children will set up their life path to become self-supportive or self-destructive by their third year. If the latter, they may separate themselves from Source. When we experience separation from the presence of God within, we separate ourselves from our pipeline to unconditional love.

As we grow up, we are not able to unwind the negatives created by aloneness, rejection, frustration, discouragement, disappointment, fear, invalidation, and guilt and humiliation until we recognize that we are all right with ourselves. Many of my clients are under the illusion that any concentrated form of attention is love, even physical abuse. As a result, a new concept of love must be established for healing to occur.

We can attempt to give clients empowering praise, strokes, support, and recognition and help them to recover their self-esteem and self-worth, but many will discount and reject validation if they feel conditions attached, or that they are not entitled. When they accept that they can release their perceived limitations (illusions) and release denial, miracles do indeed happen.

Contrary to popular belief, self-esteem is not a learned quality. It is not something you can teach someone. We all have positive, self-supporting qualities at birth as well as the innate ability to experience happiness, joy, and harmony. We were born in love and joy. As we grew up, our perceptions and interpretations of how we were treated shaped our beliefs and our view of reality

To compile a "Self-worth Inventory," we must look at the qualities that engender self-worth. I use the term "all-rightness" to encompass all the positive cluster qualities that give us the ability to feel and claim our self-esteem. They are never separated. If we have one, we will usually have all of them.

- *Self-esteem:* I feel good about myself, with no need for external validation or approval.
- *Self-love:* I recognize, support, respect, trust myself, and take responsibility, knowing my "all-rightness" without external support. I empower myself to be kind and caring of self, to follow a wellness program such as exercise and eating properly, and to listen to and respect my body.
- *Self-confidence:* I know that I can accomplish my goals; I take responsibility for them.
- *Self-approval:* I do not need anyone's approval or sanction to know that my actions are acceptable.
- *Self-acceptance:* I can be happy without another person's love, support, or acceptance.
- *Self-validation:* I am all right. Nobody has to validate me or tell me that I am all right or loved.

Very seldom do we know the base causes of dysfunction in our lives. The body is a vehicle that will always tell us our history and the truth. Every sensory input has been stored in the cellular memory. Every incident, reaction, and response that has ever happened to us is stored in our subconscious mind's video/audio recorder. Every sensory input has been recorded, along with actual voice and pictures in absolute accuracy; none are over-looked, discarded, or deleted.

When we understand the awesome power of the subconscious mind and the middle-self to disable our immune system, we will begin to recognize how disease is created. In analogy to comput-ers, the subconscious is a mainframe computer that networks with the personal cellular computers. They are able to perform only the tasks that are programmed into them. Any false beliefs, concepts, attitudes or interpretations in the system will create programs to which the body responds automatically, without conscious thought of the programmer.

Your body is your mind, and in computer language, it is also the hardware. The 'software' is any program installed in the mind. The instinctual mind is just that: if you go into survival mode, it takes over. It has no ability to think, process, or make rational de-cisions. The conscious mind is the programmer. It can also hold false beliefs and concepts of which you are unaware. If you do not question these beliefs, they will run your life.

The Conscious Rational Decision-Making Mind (CRDMM) must be on track all the time. If you "gray out" and go on auto-pilot, the inner-middle-self (IMS) can move in and take over. This operates from beliefs and does not consult the subconscious mind's computer for input very often. It will make decisions based on its interpretations which may be inaccurate.

In our work, we have experienced miracles with hundreds of people. Spontaneous releases of disease, emotional dysfunction, and genetic defects continue to amaze us. Yet many did not respond well or the dysfunction returned after a time. I soon realized that we, the healers, were not "doing" it, and that we were not "healers" or "therapists" but facilitators. We are here only to show people how to love themselves and receive love.

If you can take responsibility for your life and make that shift in consciousness, permanent healing will follow. Therapists cannot change the holographic image you hold about yourself; they can only help you make the spiritual shift, thereby causing the healing. If you cannot make that shift, the healing process will give you at best a temporary release. N/CR will work in spite of you because we are not working with your conscious mind. As a result, we are able to release old programs with 95 percent of clients.

Many times, your instinctual mind will try to keep you in survival mode, as it was originally programmed to do. In an N/CR session, we ask it to abide by our will. Since you are the script-writer, producer and director of all the shows in your life, we ask it to let you come out of the wings and take center stage. When you are the hero/heroine in your play, your subconscious mind will cooperate with you; you do this by giving the instinctual mind an affirmation.

The ego is another matter altogether. If the ego interferes, we use a different approach to make friends with your ego so that it won't sabotage you. We access the ego with N/CR and get it to recognize you as the director.

I have found that it is not the modality that causes healing to happen since many allopathic and alternative therapies have claimed provable visible healing. However, they cannot explain why remission happened or how to duplicate the process with any regularity. The effectiveness of a practitioner depends upon his or her ability to get in touch with a client's "feeling self" and establish trust so that the client feels that cared for and loved. This is what causes healing to take place. Healing is only governed by one law—the Law of Love—and it works every time. My study with *A Course In Miracles* formed part of the base, as well as *The Healing Touch* by Dolores Kregar.

Psychiatrists, doctors, psychologists, and other practitioners have long recognized the need to release negative emotions. N/CR is a controlled process that gets to the core issue. Double-blind treatments with different practitioners working with N/CR have shown that each practitioner has virtually the same experience: fear appears on the left side of the body; anger on the right; and rejection along the spine. In all, we have uncovered 60 individual locations for specific other emotional, dysfunctional programs.

In an article in *Discovery Magazine*, "A Bug in the System," scientists reported finding causes of disease but they have no cure, prognosis, or correction; they have labeled susceptibility to disease a "genetic defect." Cellular breakdown is caused by the cell's mitochondria losing their ability to process and absorb nutrients. Thus the cellular structure breaks down and the cell begins to malfunction. Often the medical explanation is that the cells die because of a genetic defect. Whatever diagnosis researchers hang on it becomes the disease. On the other hand, healing works with N/CR because it erases the cellular memory of the rejection, lack of love, etc. and helps the cell recover its original DNA blueprint, so the body begins to rebuild new healthy cells.

* * *

Whenever the subconscious files away an experience, it creates a record and program complete with energy that makes small chemical changes in the body. Each program defines how we reacted and handled the incident the first time. Then, each time we encounter this program, we reinforce the pattern with instructions on how we will handle future situations. Eventually these chemical changes cause a physical breakdown in the body. Releasing the dysfunctional emotion and the program requires understanding the cause and the reason you reacted in the manner you did.

When we understand the dialogue between your subconscious mind and your body, we can disconnect that conversation and release it. With that accomplished, we erase the program's operating instructions, destroy the patterns, and file the new record, pattern and program in the subconscious mind's archives. At this point, the energy is released and the behavior program is no longer accessible to you.

In the case of muscle pain, at the physical level, the cellular memory is released, which allows the muscle to return to its original form. The short circuit in the meridian which caused the muscle to go into contraction from emotional trauma is released. At the same time, the neural pathway patterns created from the experience are released and erased. The original program for the muscles now takes over again, and the pain is gone.

In the case of a life-threatening, dysfunctional program, the original endocrine system programs are restored, so the immune system can rebuild the "T" cells and leukocyte count to destroy the dysfunctional invading cells.

The body is a hologram in which all levels must be addressed at the same time. We must work with physical, mental, emotional, and spiritual levels simultaneously, otherwise treatment will be symptomatic and temporary. N/CR accesses the root cause because it requires the practitioner to get in contact with the client's "feeling self." By doing so, she/he can listen to information in the client's subconscious mind which has been deposited in muscles/acupuncture points by the mind. The practitioner uses acupuncture points for a switch to turn on the video/audio and allow the mind to bring the picture and experience to the front. This is where N/CR differs from other therapies. Since the N/CR practitioner listens to the client's body/mind and goes directly to base cause, we get a clear understanding of the cause of the dysfunction. By describing the situation which caused the dysfunction, then using an affirmation and asking the client to repeat it, the blockage is released.

So there is hope and recovery is possible in every case. The only catch is that you must have the desire to take control and discipline self to do what it takes. I am a walking example. My book, *Your Body Tells The Truth*, relates many case histories of people who literally shifted their belief and were healed in minutes. For some, it took days, and others showed gradual improvement over years. It all depends on how willing you are to let go of attachment to the cause and the core issues that have manifested the dysfunction. To reiterate, all causes are the same: *the root cause of all dysfunction of the body or the mind is anger, fear or rejection, which results in lack of love.* When the connection to Source is restored, or reconnected, love can begin to heal the body/mind.

The Control Addict

Need for control is the most widespread addiction we have today yet such addicts cannot recognize the symptom because the illusion and denial mask the need so perfectly that it is invisible to them. If you have an expectation or want to control a program, meeting, or another person's response, you are a control addict. You will try to control everyone and everything to get attention. As we have seen earlier, any concentrated form of attention is interpreted as love by a person who needs validation from the outside.

Many people will even hurt themselves in accidents or cause illness and disease to elicit love and attention—the so-called Münchausen Syndrome. And in the extreme, mothers will harm their children to elicit attention and sympathy from doctors and nurses (Münchausen-by-Proxy). For these people, in the absence of unconditional love, any attention will do. We will suffer or afflict abuse, both physical and emotional, to get attention. Love becomes an elusive feeling when it is conditional. Each situation is different and has myriad interpretations

As therapists, we can only guide and help our clients to understand the causes and core issues causing the dysfunction in their lives. The greatest challenge is the client who cannot receive love, or love him or herself. If love does not exist in the client's reality, how does she or he recover self-esteem and self-worth, let alone heal the self?

Explaining the cause does not change the program or pattern; it will continue on until it is released from the body and mind together. I have discovered that we can release the program/pattern from the cellular memory and the subconscious mind, yet it seems to regenerate itself again in the future when a crisis arises that relates to a belief held by the middle-self. What we have found is that the conscious mind/middle-self is divided into parts that operate under totally different conditions:

- The middle-self holds beliefs in memory that are transferred to the subconscious mind if the pattern continues. It will then create a program which becomes an operating program.
- The instinctual mind contains only beliefs that apply to survival. It works directly with the survival-self in the subconscious mind.

In the past, we assumed that clearing the programs, patterns, and records was all that was needed. Now we recognize that after we clear the programs, we have to check the middle-self to see if there are beliefs about the situation stored in its deep-level mind. The intricacies of how the mind stores information are truly amazing; we now understand how easily people bent on control can use mind control processes to affect people without their awareness of the actual contact.

There is a way out of this "Catch 22." We must commit to taking responsibility for our lives and taking our power back. Miracles do happen, and we manifest them by reconnecting with Source—the presence of God within. At this point we can accept unconditional love from self and from others. This is the primary ingredient in healing. Without love present, healing does not happen; you may get symptom relief but not true healing. That is why doctors describe a person who apparently has been cured to be in remission. You cannot cure anything. Only when you release the program and/or belief driving it will you be permanently healed.

What is Neuro/Cellular Repatterning™?

Neuro/Cellular Repatterning (N/CR)™ is a holographic, body-based psychotherapy process that uses affirmations with love and forgiveness as the basic modality. N/CR will be one of the healing processes of the future because it holds the promise of healing any dysfunction, emotional/mental problem, illness, or disease without pain, drugs, or surgery. No diagnosis is needed but only the recognition and release of the cause.

All diseases, illness, and emotional or physical breakdowns are dysfunctional behavior patterns. The delusion, denial, and irresponsibility that are part of our life cycle block us from total healing. In reality, there is no disease or illness; there is only a breakdown in our understanding what we are refusing to observe about ourselves. When we recognize the base cause and are willing to let go of it, healing can take place.

Neuro/Cellular therapy includes the use of Behavioral Kinesiology and biofeedback instruments, if necessary. We demonstrate methods to understand the dialogue, misperceptions, and interpretations the subconscious mind holds in its memory. The acupuncture points on the body are switches or gates, and putting pressure on them activates the mind's video/audio player and opens the dialogue with the subconscious mind's files.

Certain basic issues must be resolved before we can begin the process.

1. First, we must get the client anchored in his or her body. Many people are unaware that they are out of their body. If we confront a traumatic issue, the client might walk right out. Once the client senses how it feels, he or she can begin to recognize the feeling.

2. In order for kinesiology to work properly, electrical polarity must be correct. If the polarity is reversed, "yes" will appear as "no," and "no" as "yes." We cannot obtain an accurate answer until polarity is balanced properly.

3. The client has to establish an ability to allow him or herself to be loved and to love the self. Separation from Source will cause a lack of love along with rejection from self. The client must accept his/her entitlement to love.

4. We find out if the three lower minds are going to work with us. If not, then we have to rewrite and reprogram the tapes. We talk with ego to get it to recognize that we are not going to destroy it. We have to convince it to be our friend.

5. At this point, we ask questions with kinesiology or go directly into program releases. We can go directly to the root causes and the core issues stored in the subconscious mind's files. These will reveal the programs that have become the habit patterns that cause dysfunctional behavior, illness, disease, or pain in any form. N/CR can release and heal any dysfunctional program in a very short time.

All sessions are taped for the protection of therapist and client. Also, the client can choose to review the session and transcribe the affirmation. The client will be unable to remember many parts of the session as the mind may block it out. And many people find that repeating the affirmations locks in the new programming.

Questions

Q. Why is this particular process so effective?

A. Unlike other therapy processes, the client is required to participate in the session. You are not *worked on*. In most treatment
processes such as Rolfing, Trager, massage, Acupuncture, and
other body-related processes, you do not participate. In psycho-
therapy, you will be asked what your problem is, but very seldom do you know the base cause. In N/CR, the body always
reveals the base causes and the core issues if we will listen to it.
We cooperate with ego because it's one of the main players in
the game. Your ego knows exactly what's happening in your
life so we have to support it in working with you. All levels are
brought in to play. We work on all levels of physical, emotional, mental, spiritual, and etheric at the same time. The body
being a hologram, we access all levels of the mind and body.
We go one further by accessing the ability of the Higher Self.

Q. What should I expect during a treatment?

A. To understand what a treatment is like, you must first understand what it is *not* like. No special preparations are required.
You will not experience any deep tissue work that is painful,
nor will you be required to enter altered states of consciousness. We do not use hypnosis or guided imagery. You will not
be expected to dredge up painful, emotional experiences from
the past, although painful emotion may come up spontane-
ously as you experience flash-backs during the process but
they are momentary and release quickly. You do not need to
tell us anything; your body will reveal all we need to know. We
may ask some questions to establish some basic criteria.

Q. What's going on during a treatment?

A. When we locate the acupuncture point that applies to the incident we are releasing, a momentary pain will emerge at that
point. As we bring up details of the incident and forgive the
cause, it will disappear immediately. You do not experience the
mind's action during the process. It communicates to your body
in a microsecond through neuro-synapses and signals the
muscles to let go of the tension. At the same time, it is rewriting
the software programs in the computer. Through affirmations,
we communicate what we want to happen. It is important to
understand that you are giving permission and removing the

programs yourself. As you are led through the affirmation by the therapist, you are healing your own body. The therapist is actually just a facilitator who agrees to let you release the negative energy through him or her.

Q. How long does this take and how much does it cost?

A. There is no way of knowing how many treatments it will take since it depends on your willingness to let go. Taking the responsibility to see your life differently without judgment, justification, rejection or fear/anger helps. Sessions typically run 75 minutes and cost $70.

Pattern Release Process

Symptom: Mental, emotional or physical pain, depression, illness, etc. (obvious or assumed cause)

Record: Base cause interpretation of situation (subconscious mind's recording of reaction, activity or situation)

Program: Core issue (ego, subconscious mind's or sub-personalities' instructions recorded in computer, or, How I will handle situation next time.)

Pattern: Habitual Reaction—the illusion of how I have handled the situation in the past each time the stimulus arose. (addiction, control, justification, denial, authority, distortion, dishonesty, delusion.)

You can release or relieve a symptom and you may achieve remission or release of pain, but this will not cause healing to take place. You are just manipulating the energy tied up in the neurological pathway, meridian, muscle, organ, or tissue. If you do not release the cause and the core issue, the instructions will eventually cause the pattern to reassert itself when a crisis arises in your life.

The conscious mind/intellect can set up a belief and the soul can understand the process, but if the subconscious mind does not release the record from the files and lock up the operating instructions in the archives, the instructions will cause the computer to rewrite or replace the program. This will continue until the pattern, program, and record are recognized, filed, and released with love and forgiveness. Then the original cell imprint can begin operating again, healing all the dysfunctional parts of the cell.

The immune system can now regenerate at a level to allow the T-cells and leukocytes to begin doing their work again. To activate the body's healing ability, it must have access to the original blue-print. All diseases and/or emotional dysfunction will be healed by the body/mind when the programs are removed from cellular memory.

(For more information on becoming an N/CR practitioner, see Appendix A.)

12

Are You Ready?

QUITE OFTEN, WE MAKE A decision about our life path from a Conscious Mind level without recognizing that the other seven levels of our mind may have a different viewpoint on your life path. To make this quantum leap into the new millennium and the fifth dimension will take some adjustment in your way of life. It is not like just going from one year to the next, letting go of a relationship and creating a new relationship, changing jobs, or moving from one city to another. This is going to require a total shift in your viewpoint on life. Your life will not be the same nor will you be able to return to the so-called "good old days."

Very few people have got themselves ready for this shift in dimension. From 1987 to 1996, many people were becoming aware of the quickening. It seems that in 1997, people were pulling back and digging their heals in, going on auto pilot. The movement to critical mass began to slow.

I assumed, from the feeling I was getting about the consciousness shift, that we were still on track. When I began writing this book we were, but it seems that this pulling back is coupled with fear of the future.

Your mind is getting sensory input about the future changes even if you shut it off. To many people, the future looks bleak, and with this mindset, it *is* bleak. Your Middle Self operates primarily from fear until you change that mind set. It wants to protect you from any threats to your existence and will set up beliefs that will drive your life without your awareness. It assumes that it *is* protecting you, but it can only see the present and future as the past. When it gets conflicting information from your intuitive self, it will try to force you into a pattern it assumes is safe. Middle Self cannot perceive change as good but as fearful because it cannot see beyond today. It makes no difference if the present is painful or not an effective life path. It knows what today holds so that is perceived as safe.

To make this quantum jump into this new life style, we have to prepare all of our selves. When we come to the conclusion that we are run by a committee, we have to become the executive director of the committee of selves. As we integrate the separation from self, we can experience life without feeling alone, insecure, and separated. This means that you have to come to the point where you can align all levels of your mind and their sub-personalities to the same basic goal.

To make this transition means that we must release all fear-based programs and patterns. This requires a self-assessment of where we are. The first step is to list your fear- and anger-based feelings. When you do this, you must realize that what makes you angry or fearful may not be the *cause* but may only be a *result* of your feelings, interpretations, and resulting projections.

We must recognize that we are not victims. We set up our life to happen exactly the way it has turned out to the present. If it is not turning out as we would like, we can change it. We can change the future when we become aware of the past, free of illusion and denial. At this point, we can forge a new path with peace, happiness, harmony, and joy in our life by writing a new life script.

As stated earlier, after the year 2000, we will move into a new way of life. To make this transition, we must clear all our past karma and resolve all karmic contracts and karmic agreements. We must clear all the lessons that we came in to this life to learn. We must clear all the unresolved lessons with our parents because they were the main lessons we came to learn.

Most people have not cleared their childhood trauma. If you were blessed to choose parents who treated you as an individual entitled to unconditional love, acceptance, approval and supported you with a good model to help you learn, that is fantastic. Unfortunately, most of us were not but, because we want to see them in a good light, we often try to cover the pain by projecting an image that our parents' treatment of us was all right. We have to see the truth before we can accept who are parents were. When we do that, we have to recognize they did the best they could with the tools and awareness they had. Their feelings and interpretations were accurate for them at the time, no matter what they did.

You may require a third party or a therapist to help you forgive your parents and set up a new way of viewing their behavior. They did the best they could, so it is your responsibility to accept them as they were and close the doors on those lessons. When you do this with all the people in your life, you will then be ready for a quantum leap in your life to enter the New Millennium. We cannot enter the fifth dimension with unresolved issues such as this.

We have to prepare the body/mind at all levels for this new reality. You may understand at the spiritual level that we are faced with an imminent dimensional shift and earth changes, but your body/mind may not be ready.

Many of my clients have noticed that they are inexplicably warm or hot to the point of hot flashes. They have an uneasiness about the future. Some have said they are falling back into old addictions or picking up new ones. The high temperatures are caused by resistance to the quickening. The frequency shift of the earth is increasing at a faster rate now. In 1995 and 1996, it increased one hertz per year but by 1998, it increased almost two hertz in just six months. It is now at a rate of about 11 hertz. Those people who are holding back experience the increase as increased skin temperature.

Most people do not want to think or talk about preparedness for the coming changes. I have discussed this with many people who feel I am trapped in some "unreality." But look at the changes in the behavior of our politicians. If they had behaved as they do today 25 years ago, they would have run out of office in short order. But today, people just look the other way and brush it off.

This chapter may give some insights to what you may have to do to prepare yourself for the future. My books, *Your body Is Talking Are You Listening* and *Journey into the Light* provide more insight into the process of shifting and integrating your body, mind, and spirit into the new millennium.

13

Afterthoughts and Conclusion

A S CONSCIOUSNESS REACHES CRITICAL MASS, major changes will beset us. Those who are thrown into chaos by the Quickening will choose to leave, resulting in a dramatic increase in suicides and life-threatening diseases. Those who cannot move with the Quickening may actually catch on fire in spontaneous combustion. To them it will feel like being in a microwave oven; their body cells will heat up due to friction caused by the speed-up of the pace of the planet's basic energy. Friction within their dense body will cause heat to build up which may literally ignite the physical body.

According to Gregg Braden in his book, *Awakening to Zero Point: The Collective Initiation*, 64 indigenous programs operate your body yet most people have only 20 to 25 turned on. As we raise our vibrations and take control of our lives, we can activate more of these programs. My older son is a good example; his immune system is so strong that he has been sick only five days in his life, usually from emotional causes.

Also, a while ago, my feet were very dry and cracked; one crack was almost an eighth of an inch deep. When the subconscious programs were cleared, the crack healed up the next day, and a day later, I couldn't even see where the crack had been. Your body will heal itself when you remove all the programs that block you from being all right.

We will become more aware of the effects of past lives on our current lives. We really do not have to learn anything; each of us has done almost everything that has already been done so all we really need to do is remember. Our subconscious mind's computer can store and retrieve over 200,000 times more data than any computer built today.

We have all the tools at our disposal to do most anything. The problem is overcoming the dense level of reality we are in. As we increase our frequency, we will pull back the veil that blocks us from this information. As I have gone through this process, I have experienced a major awakening in my life, and within the next five years, I believe I will have reduced the density of my body such that I can walk through walls.

We will also find that what was covered up or hidden will, in the Age of Aquarius, be mysteriously discovered or reappear, such as the White House files subpoenaed by the Whitewater Committee that showed up in the White House living quarters two years later. We can also look forward to the discovery and public disclosure of the ancient records stored in the pyramids and the Sphinx, despite cover-up attempts by the Roman Catholic Church and the Egyptian Government.

We will soon live in a more ethically-based reality in which people respond with support, honesty, and integrity. Fear will no longer exist, and we will not have to protect ourselves from others who wish to cause us harm. The criminal element simply will not be able to exist on the Fifth Dimension because the frequency would destroy them.

People will break away from teachers who want to control a committed group of followers or who claim to channel Ascended Masters as a cop-out for lack of personal direction. They will say, "The masters said ...," or "That's the way we have to do it because my guidance said ...."

If you are genuinely channeling an Ascended Master, you are approaching mastery yourself and have no need of their authority.

We will be set free from false teachers who use covert fear to control their followers and students. Many people belong to organizations that do not call themselves a cult, yet the leaders require the followers to believe as they do and adhere rigidly to the rules. These groups will fall into major internal turmoil as the followers reclaim their personal power as equals. This may seem an odd prediction, yet many give their power to a leader who appears to be open but, through teachings and rules, works covertly to keep the followers disempowered. The New Millennium is about being self-actualized, yet this shift may be hard for those who want someone else to make their decisions for them.

The quantum leap into the New Millennium will also bring some major changes in the way we interact with government and the environment. For example, entitlement programs funded by government agencies will collapse under their own weight, and welfare programs will get tighter and stiffer as funding for these programs dries up. As a result, everyone will need to start carrying their own weight.

At this point, I see a major split in people's realities. While some do take control of their lives and step forward, unfortunately a majority of the population are becoming complacent sheep and stepping further into denial. There is nothing we can do for them. As Stan Deyo put it recently on the Art Bell show, *Coast-to-Coast*: "They don't really want to know what's going to happen in the future. Enjoy life now."

I am not fatalistic about the future. I see this as the most intriguing and interesting time to live in the last 2,000 years. The challenge is to prepare for the future by aligning your conscious mind and your spirit with your physical body, using the best possible methods and health.

After 2030 AD, people will have the potential to live 150 to 250 years in perfect health. I am working on the program to do so now. I am showing people that they can actually become physically younger if they use self-discipline and are consistent in their commitment to eat right, exercise, and clear all the emotional trauma/ baggage, karmic contracts, and limitations from their body/mind. It will open the door to peace, happiness, harmony, and joy. With abundance, financial freedom, and unconditional love, we can live a stress-free life which can actually reverse the aging process.

It will take committed discipline to avoid the habits and foods that destroy your physical health such as cigarettes, alcohol, and foods that have no value to your body. These habits are one of major denials to soul evolution. You can justify all you want to continue detrimental behavior, but you are the one who pays for it in the end. And emotional toxins are just as detrimental to health as sugar and white flour.

How many people will survive the quickening, the pole shift, and the move to the fifth dimension? I do not really know at this time. In 1979, I predicted a population reduction of 40 to 60 percent by the year 2012. Others have predicted from less than 10 percent to over 60 percent. It depends on how many *"get it"* as they said in EST training. Personal responsibility and committed self-discipline is the *it*. Do you have the willingness and the commitment to apply the knowledge it will take to make the shift? It is all up to you. You can lead a horse to water, but you can't make it drink.

Have a safe journey on your path to the New Millennium!

Appendix A: N/CR as a Professional Practice

Neuro/Cellular Repatterning is a body-centered, psycho-therapy process that can be a stand-alone therapy, or as an adjunct to other therapies. The medical field is describing this process as Psychoneuroimmunology. We are getting the body to talk to itself and we are reprogramming the function of the computer in the mind.

In computer terms, the body and mind are the *hardware*. The *software* is the program that is installed in the mind. The instinctual mind is just that: if you go into survival, it takes over. It has no ability to think, process, or make rational decisions. The conscious mind is the programmer. It can also hold false beliefs and concepts of which you may not be aware. If you do not question these beliefs, they will run your life. The conscious mind must be on track all the time, otherwise the ego and the subconscious mind will take over, because somebody has to be at the wheel to drive the vehicle (the body).

In all therapy processes, this question always seems to arise in the practitioner's mind:

"Am I getting to the actual programs that prevent the client from attaining the inner peace, happiness, joy, harmony, acceptance, approval and love in the client's life?"

Of course, the therapist must be in recovery him or herself, or the question wouldn't even arise. An effective therapist must be willing to confront his/her limitations and issues which may block us from becoming compassionate, non-judgmental, detached and supportive, with no need for control or authority over the outcome of the therapy.

The need for control is the most widespread addiction we have today. It is very insidious in the way we react to it, both as therapists and clients. If you are not in recovery, it is not an issue; many people in recovery do not recognize it as an issue, either. If we have an expectation or want to control a program, meeting, or a person's response, we are addicted to control.

As therapists, we are only able to guide and help a client understand the causes and core issues that are causing the dysfunction in his/her life. In the N/CR process, you cannot sidestep your own issues because they will surface along with your client's issues. In this process, you can clear many of your own issues in

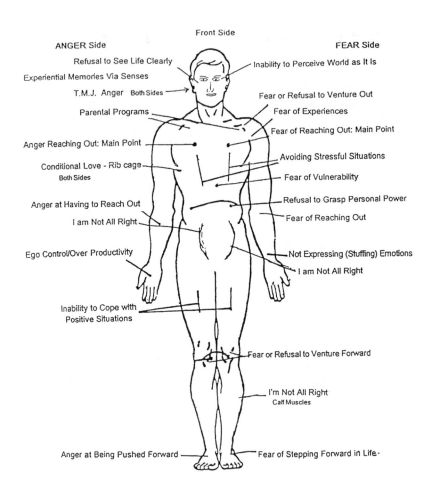

General location of energy storage—front

the therapy sessions. You will recognize them and simply release them, because you are participating with the client in the release process.

We also need to have other practitioners work with us during our recovery. We cannot read our own book well if we are attached, blocking or suppressing the causes. In my experience, even if we are committed to growth, we will block and refuse to recognize our attachment. Your body will always tell the truth, if you can get past the mind's blocks.

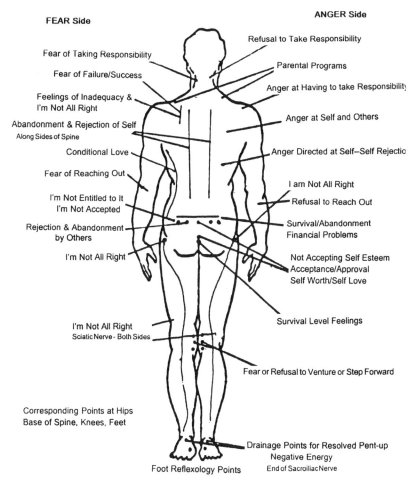

FEAR Side

ANGER Side

Refusal to Take Responsibility

Fear of Taking Responsibility

Parental Programs

Fear of Failure/Success

Anger at Having to take Responsibility

Feelings of Inadequacy &
I'm Not All Right

Anger at Self and Others

Abandonment & Rejection of Self
Along Sides of Spine

Conditional Love

Anger Directed at Self–Self Rejection

Fear of Reaching Out

I am Not All Right

I'm Not Entitled to It
I'm Not Accepted

Refusal to Reach Out

Rejection & Abandonment
by Others

Survival/Abandonment
Financial Problems

I'm Not All Right

Not Accepting Self Esteem
Acceptance/Approval
Self Worth/Self Love

I'm Not All Right
Sciatic Nerve - Both Sides

Survival Level Feelings

Fear or Refusal to Venture or Step Forward

Corresponding Points at Hips
Base of Spine, Knees, Feet

Drainage Points for Resolved Pent-up
Negative Energy

Foot Reflexology Points

End of Sacroiliac Nerve

General location of energy storage—back

The final evaluation will only come in the results a client mani-
fests, as he or she traverses the path in the journey to transformation. With N/CR, we can go directly to the root cause and the core
issues stored in the mind and locate these programs and patterns.
We use Kinesiology and the acupuncture points in the body as
gates, switches or entry points to release the information. Any dysfunctional behavior pattern, illness, disease or pain can be released
and healed a very short time through N/CR. We uncover and release the blocks to attaining self-worth, self-esteem, self-confidence,
self-validation, self-approval and unconditional love. Lack of love

is the root cause of all illness. With N/CR, one can expect to actually experience total healing in a very short time.

The major problem confronting most people today is that they cannot receive love or love themselves. If love does not exist in a person's reality, how does he or she recover self-esteem and self-worth, let alone heal him or herself? When we separate from our Source, we shut off the presence of God within.

In Level One training, we focus on effective use of Behavioral Kinesiology and listening techniques for the body/mind. We communicate through Kinesiology and intuitive listening. Verbal communication is through affirmations. When we locate the causes and core issues of the dysfunction, we communicate with specific affirmations tailored to reprogram the subconscious mind.

We have developed a body-map over the last ten years, which indicates the locations of most emotions (see above). In the last few years, we have also noticed an increase in the activity of possessive spirit beings. Five years ago, we very rarely ran into them. We have developed a very effective process to clear and release them. We can access and collect intellectual knowledge on what challenges are facing us, but we must release the base cause and core issues for healing to take place. Miracles do happen with Neuro/Cellular Repatterning.

Appendix B. Clearing Possessive Beings

On two separate occasions during 1997, when I got out of bed in the morning, I was extremely stiff. Then, this started happening every morning for about three months. When we checked the area in my lower back, we found implants. They were causing extreme pain until we removed them.

I was awakened one night by a premonition that someone or something was in my room. As I looked around, I saw three short beings standing at the end of my bed. They didn't say anything but just watched me. When I called on my Guardian Angels and the White Brotherhood, they left, simply dematerializing. This led me to believe that I was being visited and that they were trying to do something with me.

Things got quiet for about two months, until one night about 2:30 a.m. I was a awakened by extreme pain all over my body and I couldn't move a muscle even though I was fully awake. I checked to see if I was having an out of body experience or if I was astral projecting. I wasn't. At that point, I got scared and called everyone I could think on from the higher planes to help me. I then mustered as much strength as I could and jumped out bed, falling to the floor. I realized at this point that aliens had been staking me out for months and had tried to abduct me. My body had locked down every muscle in an attempt to stop them. I sensed their presence but I couldn't see them.

I got up from the floor, went into another bedroom, and chanted "Elohim" (the power name for God) for about 30 minutes. My body started to loosen up but I was unable to get back to sleep for about two hours. When I got up at seven, my body was sore all over as though I'd been beaten up. Every cell hurt. There were no obvious bruises but it felt as though there should have been. It took about three hours in a hot tub and steam room to release the pain and tightness, but it didn't finally clear up for about three days. And we had to remove yet more implants from my lower back and brain stem.

We theorized that something in me had shut my body down and tensed up every cell to protect me. A battle was going on in another dimension but I couldn't observe it for some reason. From our Source, we learned that rebel dark force Pleiadians were trying to abduct me and their own people were protecting me. It was a battle of Light versus Dark, both Pleiadian. I was astonished because I'd asked them for help before and they'd refused. I assume they helped on this occasion because their own criminal renegades were involved. I was grateful for that.

If you find yourself in a similar situation, this appendix presents you with a simple process to remove entities and their implants that can be performed by most people with very little practice. Most people have some form of entities attached to them. Getting angry, for example, gives them a way to enter. Fear-based feelings or programs also open the door. The following is a method for removing them.

A much more complex form of this process can be used to remove hidden, deactivated entities that are using masquerades or disguises. (A forthcoming book, *Clearing Aliens, Extraterrestrials, Demons, Inter-Dimensional Entities and Possessive Spirit Beings; Removing Cords, Implants, Curses, Hexes and Spells*, describes how to remove cords and implants. For a more thorough description of how to clear the causes for opening the doors, see my book, *Your Body Is Talking; Are you Listening?*)

Briefly, we use clapping hands together to loosen the entity's grip. Then we push it out using an energy-block, with your hands supplying the force. You must keep your hands on the client's body during the process of sliding them up from the feet to the head. It is very important to keep your hands in contact with the client's body.

There are two methods: a self-clearing process and one that requires a practitioner. Self-clearing is not as efficient as having another person perform the process but it does work most of the time.

Self Clearing process

1. Clap your hands behind your head then in front of your head once on each side in front and back.
2. Move down your body clapping alternatively in front and in back.
3. As you move down clapping, try to reach as high as you can on your lower back and proceed down to your legs. Clap at least three times in front and back of your legs.
4. Hit the top of your feet hard and then move up the front of your body with your hands totally in contact with your

body. As you slide your hands up, push them up and over your head in the front and in the back of your head.

5. Do this twice in the front and the back.

Practitioner process

1. Have the person lie down in horizontal position with shoes off.
2. Clap down over the body from the head to the feet.
3. Hit the bottom of the feet relatively hard, and move your hands up the body, staying in contact with the body from feet to head. If you take your hands off the body, the entity may jump back.
4. Repeat this process three times.

Appendix C: The Harmonizer

The Harmonizer is actually three models:
- An Extremely Low Frequency (ELF) device for eliminating stress, and centering and healing the body/mind connection.
- A high-frequency unit that protects against alien, extraterrestrial, interdimensional, and dark force intervention and abduction.
- A power pack that combines the above plus a programmable interface for cassette and CD players.

Through resonance, the devices generate bio-electrical fields using Tesla technology. The physical body matches itself to the stress level of its environment, and the Harmonizer counteracts the stress in your immediate vicinity, allowing your body to relax.

The Harmonizer Concept

If you take two matched tuning forks and hit one, the other one will vibrate at the same frequency. Your body does same thing. When you are subject to forms of negative vibrations or a negative or fear environment, you begin to resonate with that vibration or environment. In a stressful situation with a "flight or fight" response, the adrenal glands produce a shot of adrenaline to help you handle the situation. As a result, the body's operating frequency rises temporarily.

Once the emergency has been dealt with, the body produces nor-adrenaline and the body resumes its normal frequency. However, if you live under constant stress, survival threats, fear, or confrontative situations, you will begin to literally "live on adrenaline." This strains the adrenal glands, which in turn stresses the immune and endocrine systems.

Just as your body resonates with its environment, it will also respond to electronic devices that emit electric and electromagnetic fields. The Harmonizer is an ELF generator that radiates a frequency of 12.5 hertz (cycles per second)—the ideal frequency of a perfectly functioning body. Through resonance, the body matches this frequency and identifies with it to focus its energy and operation on perfect health. Brain chemicals such as interlukens, serratonin, and interferon all operate at 12.5 hertz. The immune and endocrine systems also work much more effectively at this frequency.

Background and History

The technology for the Harmonizer was developed by Nikola Tesla in 1906. Tesla researched electromagnetic fields and their generation by special coils. He also worked with what he called "scalar waves" (longitudinal "pressure" waves in the space-time itself). The Harmonizer generates a scalar wave field. Research has shown that the scalar wave field is the most effective way to protect the body from disruptive or disharmonic fields.

In the field of electromagnetics, the larger the coil, the stronger the field generated. The design calls for a 5,000 foot long coil plus complex electronics, which were not available in Tesla's time. But today's new computer technology has allowed us to reduce the size of the original Tesla Box to one tenth its size.

The first generation prototype of the Harmonizer had a range of about 18 inches and a battery life of 80 hours. The second generation prototype had a range of about 3 feet and a battery life of about 260 hours The sixth-generation Harmonizer had a range of about 15 feet and a battery life of over 600 hours. Today's ninth generation has a range of 27 feet and a battery life of 5,000 hours!

Theory

The following is a greatly simplified explanation of the theory behind the Harmonizer. The information that directs the various parts of the body to operate is carried by the body's neurological network, with the brain as the "switching center" that directs the information across the network to the appropriate part of the body. The network is formed of the meridian system and chemicals in the blood called neuropeptides.

Underpinning the switching center is the subconscious mind, similar to a computer, which records programs and habit patterns. All these systems must together or we will experience "software" malfunctions that manifest as anger, fear, resentment, and conflict. These eventually cause "hardware" breakdowns which we experience as illness, disease, or mental depression, etc.

Each cell is a part of the network that receives its orders from the mind through the neurological system The electrolytes and the neuropeptides in the body are the carriers. When operating properly, they maintain a delicate balance of chemicals, like the battery in your car. When they go out of balance or get run down, the electromagnetic fields break down or blow out. The body loses its ability to protect itself. Brain/mind communication breaks down and the body becomes subject to attack by diseases and outside forces.

When the physical body is in harmony, it functions at 12 to 18 hertz. However, stress and conflict cause the internal frequency to rise to 40 hertz and even 100 hertz. However, when this happens, it becomes harder for the electrolytes and neuropeptides to transmit information through the body/mind network. The rise in frequency stresses all body tissue, leading to eventual breakdown and accelerated aging. This in turn results in illness, depression, chronic fatigue, emotional instability, and disease.

The inhibited function of the adrenal glands slows the body's absorption of nutrition, causing tiredness, chronic exhaustion, and depression. As the internal frequency rises above 40 hertz, brain chemicals are no longer produced, so the adrenal glands kick in with high doses of adrenaline to keep the body functioning. This further stresses the adrenal glands, resulting in an adrenaline deficiency and chronic depression, which the medical profession treats with Prozac or Valium. These "feel good" drugs are addictive because they signal to the brain that the system-wide malfunction is a false alarm, so the situation is allowed to continue. (For more information about how diseases and illnesses affect the body, see my book *Your Body Is Talking: Are You Listening?*)

The Low Frequency Harmonizer

The LF Harmonizer balances all the electrical, metabolic, and electromagnetic systems that are dysfunctional by shutting out the disharmonious stress that causes the body to increase its frequency. By encouraging the body's systems to resonate at their optimum frequency, it strengthens those systems.

Most devices, plants, and animals have positive and negative energies that rotate clockwise and counterclockwise. This creates a balance in their electrical systems. A few plants, such as garlic, onion and some herbs, radiate a double positive field, hence their antibiotic, healing qualities.

The LF Harmonizer also radiates a double positive field: an ELF field of 12.5 hertz (the new Earth frequency). When within this 15 foot diameter field, your body will assume this frequency and you will notice that your body begins to relax as your organs and endocrine system begin to operate at their optimum level. Depending on the individual, maximum relaxation could take up to a week. However, within a week, your body will become accustomed to the optimum frequency and you will notice a general sense of well-being.

It must be noted that the LF Harmonizer is simply an aid, and is no substitute for proper nutrition and cannot counteract abuse of the body. Whilst the device may catalyze miraculous healing, the user also has a large part to play in a successful restoration of balance.

In operation, the Harmonizer will loosen up stuck feelings and toxins in the body. When they surface, you may experience conflicts in your life. If this happens, it's a signal to take stock of what's happening and work through it.

The High Frequency Harmonizer

The High Frequency Harmonizer operates at 9.216 MHz (the frequency of the Ark of the Covenant!). Apparently, this is a universal frequency that repels all negative energy such as that of extraterrestrial, interdimensional, and dark force intervention, attack, abduction, cording and implantation.

The HF unit duplicates all functions of the LF unit but since it operates in a different way, it provides many other features, including some that surprised even the designer. It appears that the device somehow (and theoretically impossibly) emits a scalar wave in the fifth dimension that acts as a barrier to negative energy, be it earthbound or extraterrestrial. The signal also accelerates the body's healing by activating cellular regeneration at a rate ten times the norm.

Trying to combine both units initially resulted in a unit that was too bulky to be carried on the belt or in a purse, which is why we developed the third unit for therapeutic work. It emits a very powerful signal for 15 mintues and then automatically drops down to a lower signal level. This is useful for the practitioner who wants to clear attached spirits or alien entities before continuing with the therapy.

Testimonials

Under current FDA regulations, no claims can be made as to what the Harmonizer can accomplish. Nor can we diagnose, prescribe or even recommend the device. However, we can report on feedback from users over the last four years.

In my own case, a chain-saw wound simply hadn't healed in months, but as soon as I had the HF unit with me, it healed completely in just two weeks. Watching the wound knit together and create new tissue was just like watching a "freeze frame" movie.

Many have reported that it pulled them out of depression within five days and, as a result, they were able to stop taking mind-altering prescription drugs. Chronic Fatigue Syndrome sufferers report a total reversal of their condition within a week, with a feeling of overall well-being and an increased ability to handle stress.

Many also report that they are calmer and not as easily angered. In fact, licensed psychiatrists have told us that the Harmonizer alleviates depression because it restores normal brain chemistry. Other users report clearer thinking, and improved decision-making and memory. Meditations are also found to be more vivid and effective.

At a physical level, users have reported accelerated healing, such as a broken bone that fully mended in just four weeks (one third of the time estimated by a doctor.)

House plants that are close to dying revive in one or two days when placed in the Harmonizer's field.

A client simply could not hold the unit in his hand no matter how hard he tried, so I held it while it cleared him of all his attached beings. Thereafter, he could hold it without problem.

A healer was constantly plagued by entities she would pick up from her clients. Today, she cannot imagine working without her Harmonizer.

To Order

The current ninth-generation device is about the size of a pager, with a range of about 27 feet and runs for 5,000 hours on four rechargable AA batteries. It is priced at $295. Stocks of the previous model (range of 15 feet, and runs on a 9-volt battery for 400 plus hours) have been reduced from $250 to $95.

To order a Harmonizer or for more information, contact The Wellness Institute, 8300 Rock Springs Rd, Penryn, CA 95663 or call 1-800-655-3846 or 1-916-663-9178.

Appendix D. Future Prophesy

The following were predicted in 1978-1981. During this period, I was amazed that information was so easy accessible and that there seemed to be no limitation as to content.

To lock into the Akashic record, you must first make sure you have the right "station" and the proper "telephone operator." (There are spirit guides out there from the dark forces with a lot of false and inaccurate information who would love to convince you that they are the source you want to talk with.) Even legitimate guides cannot lower their frequency to our third-dimensional level to communicate with us, so we must learn to elevate our consciousness level to theirs.

1. By the year 2012, we will see a reduction of the population of this planet by 40 to 60 percent through civil war, famine, plague, earthquake, flood, and diseases that defy our medical ability to cure. This has already started.

2. There will not be a third world war despite what many believe. However, I do see a number of regional localized wars.

3. Communism will fall as a major political force in the next ten years. (This has already happened.)

4. Medicine as we know it now will disappear by the year 2020. The process will no longer be symptom-oriented but will focus on base cause and core issues that cause disease and illness. Alternative forms will be at the forefront, working with body/mind and spirit. This will begin to happen before the end of the century.

5. By 2015, life spans will increase to between 150 and 200 years as stress, competition and the need for control become things of the past.

6. Religion will shift from ruling by fear to guiding people. The organized religions that hold power over people will cease to exist as we know them. We will see a major change in the Christian religion with its separatist views. As its influence begins to wane, it will shift to accept all religions. As Christians become aware that their view of the second coming of Christ and the rapture are not going to happen, they will become more accepting of other religious views. Of course, the radical religious fanatics will always hold on to the old views, but they will be in the minority and will eventually fade out.

7. Governments will go through a major shift as they return power to the people. Local control will increase and as the population reorients to increased personal responsibility. Federal government will be more than halved in size, and the political structure as we know it today will cease to exist.

8. Will the Christ as we knew him return, as many of the religious prophesies foretell? No. The Christ force will manifest in us as a whole, so many people will wait in vain for the second coming. Thus, the transformation of this planet is your hands. The Christ energy will manifest through anyone who has the eyes to see and the ears to hear. Many people will achieve ascension into lightbody, not through lifting of karma or some divine revelation, but by taking responsibility for one's own lesson in life, through discipline, commitment, intention, and consistent action.

9. Many false prophets, shamans, gurus, and spiritual teachers will arise, claiming to have the message and that they are the leaders of the new age. We will see self-proclaimed spiritual teachers on every street corner. However, these false teachers will fade away by the year 2015. During the period 1995 to 2000, true teachers will also come forth, recognizable by their detachment from any need for validation for their work. They will not lead but show the way, advocating self-empowerment.

10. The predicted earth changes will be modified. A major shift in 1987 will shift the consciousness of the people, and this will trigger a new form of predictions. The power of people's thought will be able to shift a predicted disaster. Many of the predicted changes will still happen, but not the catastrophes that have been predicted. The pole shift will occur but not at nearly as severely as was predicted, due to the consciousness of the population rising and modifying the changes.

11. Time as we know it will speed up. (Of course, this will be evident only to those who have can recognize it.) It will be accompanied by a quickening of consciousness that will affect people's stress level. Resisting the evolution of consciousness causes friction that results in people physically heating up.

Appendix E. Present Predictions

When making predictions about the future, we must be very careful about the sources we listen to. In a recent disturbing phenomenon, many people would rather not have to deal with earth changes and the accompanying financial and economic upheaval. They would like to believe that a benevolent God or some alien group is going to intervene and take care of everything.

People throw this information out as though they channeled some authoritative unimpeachable source. In fact, they get upset when their veracity is questioned. One problem is that we have been invaded by many rebel alien groups who want to become sources of channeled information. But their agenda is to misdirect, sabotage, and control. They are so insidious that they can slip in and displace an honest, clear source very easily if we are not vigilant. And by giving us information we want to hear, it is easy for them to masquerade as a true source.

With rebel groups of Pleiadians and Andromedans entering the picture with their advanced technology that allows them to control communication, it is all the more important to question and identify our sources. Otherwise, we feel as if we are right and can be confident that we have dialed into the true source. Their intent, however, is to disarm us and make us feel comfortable so we let go of the fear of the shifts that are taking place. And this puts us in denial of denial.

If you were to ask their Holographic Mind, you would get an accurate answer, Unfortunately most people are driven and directed by the middle-self and the Conscious Irrational mind even though they will deny it. So we have a Catch 22. We are asking a mind that does not want to tell the truth and also wants to be in control of your life. Our inner auto pilot runs off its stored programs, not from wisdom and knowledge. So, we have a basic denial program running our behavior. How can we possibly get an accurate answer?

The trap is that we can be deluded into thinking we can feel more safe and secure when, in fact, this feeling comes from a "denial of denial" program. Unfortunately, most people have a subpersonality that is in denial of the truth when it comes to earth changes. They would rather not think about and plan for a major disaster. When people tell me that they are contact with extraterrestrials who assure them that they are some supernatural force here to save us from upcoming disasters, they are supporting this attitude of denial. People want to believe these so-called saviors without reservation because they are now relieved from having to take control of their lives, reclaim their personal power, and take responsibility. This co-dependent attitude is the illusion of the times we are living in and is one of the reasons that we are devolving on this planet.

The lesson here is discernment and becoming aware that *the march of time is Quickening and is not going to change unless we change.* We must not continue to assume that some external agent is going to intervene to change the progress of time as we have done for thousands of years. Look where this thinking has got us: the destruction of Atlantis and Lemuria, world wars, religious wars, wanton killing of people who did not follow the truth of the Roman Catholic Church, and separation to the point that many believe the earth is only 6,000 years old and that Christianity and Jesus Christ are the only way to heaven.

We cannot even see how to reclaim our personal power. Many people would rather let *Big Brother Government take care of them and give up their freedom for the benefits.* Many people feel the new world order would make travel, commerce, and financial transactions simpler if we had one currency. And that crime would be reduced and medical health improved if we had a chip implanted in our bodies that held our medical history and would allow us to be tracked. Yes, it would definitely be simpler, but imagine the control this would give government. And what about all the myriad laws that could then be imposed to limit our freedom.

On the other hand, many people blow fear of earth changes out of proportion, trumpeting the old, out-dated predictions that have since been modified by the shift in consciousness over the last two decades. Such people give power to those who say, "Look at all the fear that was generated by these predictions. Few of them have happened so they are not accurate."

With this ammunition, the counter forces call the fear predictors false prophets when, in fact, the predictors were more right than the challengers who claim that everything is all right and the risks have been overcome. The true challenge is discernment because both of them are right to some extent. Yes, the earth changes have been moderated and will not be as disastrous as predicted, but they are far from being eliminated. Yes, earth changes will still happen, but they continually shift by our rising consciousness. Of course, many will continue to stick their heads in the sand and say, "I am just one person. What can I do?" Continue their denial, probably.

Let me update my future predictions, as of July, 1998:

1. THE Y2K situation. Major computer problems will occur with computer systems that abbreviate the year to two digits and cannot handle the "00" year. Most computer crashes will happen when business opens on January 3, 2000. Hardest hit will be financial institutions, since the clearing houses will not be able to process checks or ATM and credit card transactions, and few banks nowadays operate manually with no connections going through a mainframe computer. It will be important to have enough cash on hand for at least two weeks to a month. Please be prepared.

2. Most government agencies cannot upgrade their computer systems in time, and bringing everything up-to-date will take from two to ten years. If you are depending on the government for anything, it will be delayed. On the other hand, we have sufficient information available from the same Sirian and Pleiadian sources that provided most of the technologies for today's computers. However, the same control issues still exist within our power structures that have been responsible for breakdowns in the past. The know-it-alls have to be in control, and if they did not design it, then it couldn't possibly work. So those who must be in control of everything are not open to the possibility that there may be a solution. As a result, they are closed to information from extraterrestrials. The latter, therefore, have decided to let us figure the problem out ourselves. Of course, they could relent.

3. We have not reached zero point yet. This will come sometime between March 12 and May 5, 2000. At that point, the poles will begin to shift. How dramatic this is will be determined by whatever shifts we make in our consciousness by that time.

4. Earth changes will continue with global temperature increases, causing power outages, crop failures, and many

health problems. Other areas will experience the opposite effects, with floods, tornadoes, and hurricanes. Earthquakes will intensify after the pole shift, but a more immediate problem will be volcanic eruptions around the Ring of Fire. California will not become submerged and sink into the ocean. The tectonic plate movement is still happening but at a slower rate. All the changes I predicted earlier are still in force.

5. The El Nino effect is shifting weather patterns all over the planet. There is a definite possibility that temperature increases will affect the Antarctic ice. Most of the planet's ice mass is at the South Pole, and its melting will throw the balance of the planet off further, causing an imbalance that will dislodge the shelves. One ice shelf, the Larsen B, has already cracked and a huge iceberg has already broken away. Shelf break-up and melting will cause a rise in the ocean level of between 20 and 400 feet. This is significant because 3 billion people live within 50 miles of a coastline.

6. The reduction of population will definitely continue with infectious diseases, AIDS, and other causes such as localized wars. A global plague will begin after the year 2000. Another main cause of reduction will be self-inflicted, such as heart attacks and respiratory diseases. Many other people who are in denial of denial of their fear of the future will just walk out or pass on with no assignable disease syndrome.

7. Many people want to believe that everything is all right so that they can go on with their pseudo-happiness in denial of present and future conditions. Otherwise, we would see tremendous emotional breakdown and depression. This in turn would cause problems in business and government as many employees would be unable to do their jobs.

8. Contrary to the current political/military mind set, we will not have a third world war. Thinking people are fed up with war and will stop any major war buildup. However, unstable countries, where control and anger are still major issues, will experience local wars. Their purpose will be to gain control or power, rather than to liberate the oppressed.

9. Alternative therapies and medicine will gain a foothold and take over the medical care field by 2015. Practitioners will

function as therapists to help people see the denial that causes disease. Denial of denial is the major cause of disease and illness.

10. As the age of reason, ethics, love and forgiveness comes into full force, the population's stress level will decrease and life spans will increase.

11. Religions as we know them will disappear and be replaced by more of a philosophy of life, with groups working together rather than separately as we see now. We will move into an age of acceptance rather than rejection of other's views.

12. Centralized government will dissolve as people begin to return to local, grass-roots control of their lives and actions. This will eventually evolve into a loose federation which one could equate with the new world order but without central control as people will work together. Bureaucracy as we know it today will disappear, to be replaced by a political structure in which people will give one to five years of their time on a part time basis to work in state governments. Local governments will be very limited in size since citizens will donate their time to run many local functions.

13. We will see a temporary increase in the number of false prophets as rebel aliens using mind control convince them that they have the answers. Most of those channeling rebel Pleiadians will deny that fact, claiming instead to have "the truth." Unfortunately they truly believe what they are saying, yet they are living in an illusionary reality. As the Christians say, "The devil can perform miracles too." So it makes no difference what you are channeling. The only possible reality is how well your discernment operates in relation to the truth. There is only one truth, but we must be clear in order to understand it. Many people are following fundamentalist conservative church leaders out of fear as a group, and many "store front" church groups are springing up to cater to their fear. History records that this always happens in times of uncertainty and strife so that people can have some group to belong to. To be or feel alone is very fearful, and there is safety in a group you can identify with. It

is a basic human tribal instinct, and group members believe that they are coming together for social, philosophical and religious reasons. But deep down, the groups are promoting denial of denial.

14. Spiritual teachers who are teaching the truth will begin to emerge during 1999. The new teachers will advocate reclaiming your power. They will ask people to empower themselves and not rely on anyone as an outside authority, but accept themselves as their source of power. They will stand out because they will not claim themselves as the way. They will be detached from needing validation to demonstrate their work. The shamans and the spiritual leaders of the past will have to adhere to this new way of life or they will fade out.

15. As the quickening accelerates, people will either get in step with the shift or they will begin to experience depression and chronic fatigue that will render them unable to function in life. This began around 1990 and we are seeing increasing numbers of people who are unable to cope. Those that can handle the shift will sleep less, gain more energy, and have more success in their life. However, we cannot measure our own level of evolution because it is human nature to give yourself a false reading. We always want to see ourselves as accomplishing what we want. Of course, on the opposite side of this are those people who see themselves as never accomplishing what they want and as a result are rejecting themselves.

The march of the Quickening is on. Are you ready to step on the path for this journey into the new, exciting world of the next millennium? To jump out of the nest, spread your wings, and fly. This is the lesson of Jonathan Livingston Seagull.

Happy flying.

About the Author

After a very troubled beginning, about the age of eight, Art's childhood smoothed out and he appeared to be well adjusted. But, there was an undercurrent that he did not understand. He seemed to be able to succeed at whatever he turned his hand to, yet couldn't seem to sustain the success. His self-esteem and self-worth were very low, and nobody could understand why. He found school-work very easy, getting above average grades with very little study.

After five years of college, he became frustrated, feeling that it wasn't taking him where he wanted to go. He entered the business field in 1963, looking for his vocation but left in 1968 to rebuild a winery/vineyard that had been a bootleg winery during Prohibition. He sold the winery in 1975 and built a restaurant, which he operated until the end of 1977, when he returned to college for a degree in psychology. He claims, however, that he has learned more about human behavior from working with his clients in his practice than he has in any classroom setting.

Also in 1977, Art began examine some aspects of his life that puzzled him, something that would consume him for two decades.

His search culminated during a 1986 Dick Sutphen seminar when he underwent a walk-in regression and found that he was one of seven walk-ins at the seminar. All seven were over 40 years old and had been walk-ins for many years without even knowing when it had happened. Most had walked in during a traumatic accident or near-death experience. Apparently, Art had walked into the body of an eight-year-old boy who had been in a coma for six days following surgery for a ruptured intestine. The boy had been given a one-in-ten chance of surviving. To the amazement of the doctors, he walked out of the hospital three days later, totally healed.

Apparently, the body's original occupant had been a loner with very few friends. He was left-handed and wrote backwards. He couldn't read very well since the schoolbooks appeared reversed to him. This left him with severe dyslexia. After the walk-in during the hospital stay, young Art could read and write perfectly.

During the seminar, Art discovered that, before walking into the body of the unhappy eight-year-old boy, he had defined a specific mission for the incarnation, yet it would take him ten years to clear the negative programming he had inherited from the previous occupant.

Although blessed with a strong body, it began to degenerate quickly and he was told by doctors that he would end up in a wheel chair in the future if his body continued to break down. So in 1958, Art began to search for a healing modality that would heal his body. During the 20-year search, he tried all forms of medicine and many alternative therapies.

The search yielded little until 1978 when, in a workshop with Ronald Beesley, Art discovered part of the answer: that our bodies store our life's negative experiences in the muscles. Beesley was able to remove the pain that had been with Art 24 hours a day for 17 years.

In subsequent training in spiritual psychology with Paul Solomon, he began his search for a healing modality that would totally clear his physical pain. He studied homeopathy, aryuveda, Chinese and Tibetan medicine, and many of the alternative therapies, including healing processes of the kahunas and Essenes, trying to find a process that would heal his body. By 1982, he realized that the actual base cause of any dysfunction had to be cleared before he could heal anything. This led him to develop **Neuro/Cellular Repatterning**

(N/CR). The history and development of this process is fully described in Art's book, *Your Body Tells The Truth*.

A chiropractor who had known Art for many years was skeptical that all the healing he claimed to have taken place could be true; the physical dysfunction that was present 20 years earlier had been too severe. At his expense, he performed a full body X-ray, and to his utter amazement, Art's claims proved to be true. The only problem left was a minor wedging of the fifth lumbar which has since been healed.

In addition to his work with N/CR, Art has been communicating with the **Source** since December 11, 1978. They are with him when he is writing, giving direction. Most of the time he feels as if he is merged since he receives the material via his own thought process, but he is actually writing material about which he has no prior knowledge.

Art has recently taken on a new responsibility. He and Bernard Eakes have confronted the Dark Forces directly in a move to clear the planet of their control. They have found that everyone has some form of attachment with Dark Forces; it can be checked very easily with muscle testing. Art and Bernard invite anyone who desires to help them in this adventure to contact them. They will teach people how to use the clearing process that they have developed to clear people of implants and other intervention by the Dark Forces. Training is necessary since before working with others, practitioners must first be clear themselves.

Since 1965, Art has been in a working partnership with his wife, Susie. They have two sons, Ross and Ryan.

Art travels extensively, presenting lectures, seminars and workshops on N/CR, how to access the Akashic Record, and on his books: *2011: The New Millennium, Being a Spiritual Being in a Physical Body, Journey Into The Light,* (a manual on ascension), and *Your Body is Talking; Are You Listening?* He visits a regular circuit of cities each month for personal sessions. You can contact him through the Wellness Institute.